Signed by: Joan James-Reid
Author & Publisher

Published By: Joan James-Reid

"Marriage Is Under Fire – Don't Stop Firing Back!"

Edited By: Kerri-Ann Haye-Donawa @ Conclusio House,
Brampton, Ontario Canada
www.conclusiohouse.com

Copyright C 2016 by Joan James-Reid

Printed BY: Printing Icon – Markham, Ontario, Canada
info@printingicon.com
*All Rights Reserved
ISBN: 978-0-99580-550-7
Details on how to obtain copies of this manuscript – contact
Author: Joan James-Reid
Website Address: marriageisunderfire.com
Telephone Number: 289-401-0957
Email: marriageisunderfire@gmail.com

Cover designer: Bryan McFarlane
FOREWORD: Dr. Lennox D. Walker
Endorsement: Dr. George S. Peart
Interior design: Bryan McFarlane
Author Photographed by Magenta Photo Studio

This manuscript shall not be reproduced in parts nor in whole. Prior written permission must be obtained from the publisher, Joan James-Reid for the reproduction of this manuscript, either by electronic means, recording, mechanic or any other such format. Please don't indulge in or be party to the violation of the Author's rights. Only authorized copies can be sold.

Canadian ISBN Publishers' Directory
Library & Archives of Canada
"Marriage Is Under Fire – Don't Stop Firing Back!"
ISBN #: 978-0-995-80550-7

If while journeying through the pages of this manuscript, you find any similarities between the material covered here and any person or persons you might be acquainted with, be cognizant of the fact that its contents are purely based on the word of God.

Marriage Is Under Fire: Don't Stop Firing Back!

Letter of Endorsement

The prospector, be it of gold or diamond, often searches far and wide, digs deeply for long periods of time, and often finds nothing. However, every once in a while he's rewarded with a rare find, enough to reward him for the many fruitless hours of searching. Such is the gem found in this book, Marriage Is Under Fire: Don't Stop Firing Back!

It is a rare find, because the writer has the courage to open up the Pandora's box of the unknown, because one can only know the secrets of marriage from the inside, and most people are either unwilling or too ashamed to share with the public the private experience of a failed marriage.

The writer has given the reader an insightful look at marriage from both the human perspective and God's perspective, something that is missing among much of the literature on marriage today. A rare find indeed.

Come, take the journey with me. You are going to enjoy it!

Dr. George S. Peart

DEDICATION

I want to dedicate this book to my loving and virtuous mother, who epitomizes the virtuous woman described in Proverbs 31. Indeed, "her price is far above rubies." Truly, her children, grandchildren, great grandchildren, and those who have come in contact with her call her blessed. I want to also dedicate this book to those persons who are preparing to take this lifelong journey of marriage and those who are currently married. Lastly, for those who have already embarked on this journey but whose train has been derailed along the way by circumstances, or maybe hitchhikers, be encouraged, God is still in control. If that sounds like you, just cast your cares upon the Lord, and He will sustain you.

ACKNOWLEDGEMENTS

To the late Elsie Miller, a warrior of faith who has fought a good fight, ran this race with much patience, and has kept the faith to the end. Acknowledgement is also due to my current bishop, Dr. Lennox D. Walker of Praise Cathedral Worship Centre, whose unwavering faith and perseverance have inspired me to hold on, even during the most challenging situations. You have been instrumental in the furtherance of my spiritual growth, development, and my tenacity to persevere to the end. One of your most admirable qualities is a forehead that is synonymous to a flint.

Thank you to Pastor Ashvern Thompson at Green Pastures Full Gospel Church in Trelawny, Jamaica. You, too, have helped me greatly on this journey. Also, thank you to other ministers of the gospel, including Dr. George Peart who gave such a powerful endorsement for this book. To the saints of God who have sown into my life in a very inspirational manner, your encouragement and prayers have not gone unnoticed. To those who have given a word of encouragement and have also prophesied into my life, I want to say thanks to all of you. Your involvement in my life is very much appreciated

To my dear husband, Lary, who was very instrumental in getting the technical component of this manuscript completed. You have been a tower of strength to me with continuous prayerful support. I am extremely grateful for this.To my two daughters and granddaughter, you are all so dear to me. I love you all so deeply. Also, to my six siblings, one of whom departed from this life in August 2016. You have all stood by me while I walked through the valley. I do love and appreciate you all. Barry, you are gone but not forgotten. You will always be in our hearts. My loving nieces and nephew, you are not forgotten.

FOREWORD

I am Dr. Lennox D. Walker, Administrative Bishop for the Church of God in Eastern Canada. Also, the Senior Pastor for Praise Cathedral Worship Centre in Mississauga, Ontario Canada for over seventeen (17) years.

In addition, I have served on the Regional Council of the Church of God in Ontario, District Overseer for the Mississauga District and Co-ordinator for the Ministerial Internship Program (MIP) in Eastern Canada. I have also served on the National Pastor's Advisory Council in Cleveland, Tennessee and is a humble recipient of the Queen's Diamond Jubilee Medal in 2012 by Queen Elizabeth 11. This was awarded to me for exceptional work done in shaping lives in Western Mississauga, specifically.

I have done a perusal of the main components of this rare gem, in the form of this manuscript, entitled *"Marriage Is Under Fire – Don't Stop Firing Back!"* As a result of this, I have acquired a very good knowledge of its contents and purposes

The *Author, Joan M. James-Reid* has been known to me personally, for over seventeen (17) years. This is due to the fact that she has been a very dedicated member of Praise Cathedral Worship Centre, of which I have been the Senior Pastor from the year 2000 to present. She has also served on the Outreach Team of this local church for some time. Joan is currently a faithful member of the Sanctuary Choir.

As her Pastor, I do have a close and considerable involvement with Joan James-Reid and her family in different capacities. These include Family and Marriage Counselling, and christening of her beautiful grand-daughter. I also proudly officiated at her wedding as she got joined to Larry M. Reid in marriage.

Joan James-Reid is most fitting to write this manuscript in so many ways. **Firstly**, her invaluable practical experiences and insights about marriage have qualified her to write about this very important subject matter. **Secondly**, as a dedicated woman of faith and her wealth of knowledge of the word of God. **Thirdly**, Joan's passion for the preservation of the Family Unit. She has an inclination and tenacity to restore and prevent this unit from this moral decay that it is currently facing. Hence, she desires to equip and empower individuals to become better spouses. One of her goals is to become a licenced Psychotherapist, specializing in Marriage and Family Christian Counselling. In this case, she will be better able to mold and transform lives, based on the words of God.

There are many benefits to be derived from reading through the pages of this manuscript. The author has done exceptionally well in addressing these many problems that this covenant relations faces and she has provided some important tools that can be used in addressing these problems.

It will in fact benefit a total broad sweep of individuals, namely those who have a natural inclination to get married, those who are currently married and those who have embarked on this life-long journey but have suffered some misfortune along the way.

For those who are planning to get married, it will help you to prepare for this journey. This will also prevent you from entering into marriage in a state of un-preparedness. Those persons who are currently married will find some invaluable tools to improve on having a successful marriage. There are also vital information for those who have suffered misfortune along the way, in that the information contained in this, will shed much light on what might have gone wrong and how to prevent it from re-occurring.

There are some very important points that stand out vividly in this manuscript. The author makes it clear that the love that a man should have for his wife should mirror or be parallel to the love that Christ has for His Church. She took the time to pinpoint God's intended purposes for marriage and the various missiles being launched against it. Much emphasis is placed on sex and intimacy which are integral parts of marriage and should not be a taboo.

I want to give you a brief synopsis of this manuscript. Its central theme is that of marriage as a covenant relationship and the tactical approaches which are being used to destroy it. For example, efforts made to re-define marriage, adultery, abuses etc. It unravels God's purposes for marriage and the principles surrounding its existence and fruitfulness.

Here, the author identified the major foundational components of marriage. These are love, trust and reciprocity. Reciprocity here is contextualized as give and take, but in the sense of a spouse extending grace, mercy and forgiveness to each other. This is in the case where one offends the other. Let's face it as humans, offences will come in your marriage; but how you deal with it makes a big difference.

The author, Joan James-Reid offered some of the necessary tools to be used in counteracting these missiles which are being used against marriage. Therefore, enabling you to be victorious in this battle. Don't loose sight of the fact that this is a spiritual battle that is designed to destroy the Family Unit. Whenever the Family Unit is broken down, the Kingdom of God suffers violence, but you have to be deliberate and take it back – by force. This also has a chain reaction on society on a whole. It also suffers whenever this unit is destroyed.

This manuscript is quite effective in fostering positive changes and can be used in Marriage and Family Counselling, Churches, Singles and Couples' Ministry, Seminaries etc.

In closing, I want to remind you that I take much pride in writing this FOREWORD for this a God-inspired and God-centered manuscript, because this is meant to foster positive behavioral changes towards the sanctity of marriage. It is designed to bring about an awakening. I do see the need for the restoration of the sanctity of marriage in our churches and society in general.

Marriage is a covenant that should not be put asunder, except under one condition and that is infidelity. It is deeply intertwined in love, sacrifice and commitment to each. It is not one-sided. Also, the love that a man has for his wife should mirror the love that Christ has for His church.

As a Minister of the Gospel, by virtue of my position, I am a Life-changer and the contents of this manuscript is in fact life-changing and includes a total broad sweep of individuals. These include those who have a natural desire to get married, those who are currently married and those who were married but have experienced some misfortunate along the way.

Therefore, I implore you to take some time and carefully read the pages of this manuscript. As you read, pay close attention to its contents and its instructions. I strongly believe that you will greatly benefit from doing that as you propel into action. You will not be disappointed that you did. Whenever you find something that is this valuable and helpful, endeavour to share it with others.

DR. LENNOX D. WALKER.
Administrative Bishop for the Church of God, Eastern Canada & Senior Pastor for Praise Cathedral Worship Centre, Mississauga, Ontario.

TABLE OF CONTENTS

	Foreword	
	Introduction	1
Chapter 1:	The Definition of Marriage	4
Chapter 2:	The Purposes of Marriage as Designed by God	10
Chapter 3:	The Missiles Against Marriage	19
Chapter 4:	Ways to Keep Firing Back to Win the Fight	29
Chapter 5:	Dangers of Unforgiveness in Marriage	42
Chapter 6:	Benefits of Forgiveness in Marriage	46
Chapter 7:	Fighting Back	48
Chapter 8:	Warnings to the Married and Unmarried	57
Chapter 9:	Words of Caution to Men and Women	61
Chapter 10:	Abuse in Marriage	65
Chapter 11:	The Sanctity of Marriage	70
	Conclusion	73
	Author Biography	75

INTRODUCTION

The contents of this book may be considered explosive to some, so fasten your seatbelt for a truthful ride. As you journey through the pages of this book and its contents, you may experience some discomforts and may need to make changes in your approach to this covenant relationship. It will cause you to re-examine what you thought you knew about the covenant of marriage and its sanctity. It may propel you into making the necessary adjustments for a more fruitful union.

God specifically stipulated for us in Exodus 20:14 that marriage is indeed sanctified and should be upheld as such. Sex and marriage are held in high esteem in the Scriptures, and have been sanctified by God. In the book of Genesis, the first marriage was conducted after God made man and saw that he was lonely. He also saw that it was not good for him to be alone, therefore he formed woman. After He formed woman from the rib of the man, God then brought the woman to the man. This is clearly indicating the fact that God's intent for marriage is a covenant between a man and a woman. A man and a woman were only brought together in marriage, the sacred union. Oh, what a beautiful thing this is meant to be. However, it is not regarded this way by many people today.

From a biblical standpoint, it is proven that one of the primary purposes of marriage is companionship. God provided the solution to man's loneliness by forming woman. Another purpose for which marriage was designed is the procreation of the human race. Marriage was also meant to prevent fornication. That is why the Bible clearly stipulates that a woman should have her own husband, and a man should not envy his neighbour's wife (1 Corinthians 7:2; Exodus 20:17). Simply put, get and take care of your own spouse. Don't allow your neighbour's grass to be greener than yours, and don't allow yourself to envy your neighbour's grass. If this is the case, there is a maintenance issue. The solution is simple—go and water your own grass so that it can be greener than your neighbour's, or just as green.

Last, but not least, is the issue of leaving and cleaving and becoming one flesh. Ultimately, marriage is designed to bring God glory. It is a portrait that mirrors God's love and commitment to His Church. He loves His Church so much that He gave His life for it. The Church in turn must love God and submit herself to Him. He is the Bridegroom and the Church is His Bride. Similarly, as God is the Bridegroom of His Church, the husband is the bridegroom in a marriage. He should love his wife likewise. The wife, like the Church to Jesus Christ, should submit herself to her husband.

This involves intimacy between a man and his wife, emotionally, physically, and spiritually. Their two hearts should beat as one; two flesh becoming one. Currently, the sanctity due to marriage is totally being disregarded. Instead, cohabitation without marriage is being embraced by many in our society. This sacred covenant is being desecrated, over and over, without any remorse by many. It is being fired on immensely.

This book is intended to revolutionize your thinking about the honour that must be given to marriage. This union is indeed under intense fire, but endeavour to keep firing back. The war to destroy marriage will not be victorious. This sinister plot is meant to redefine marriage, to divert it from God's intended purpose, and to ultimately destroy this union. Let us all pledge before God to win this fight for our marriages, so that God can be glorified. To those who have already been embracing the sanctity of marriage, I encourage you to continue doing so. This is God's will.

This book is about the covenant relationship of marriage and the missiles that are being launched against it. It specifically speaks about the campaigns orchestrated against marriage to desecrate its sanctity. Keen attention is given to explaining what God's purposes for marriage are. These purposes include procreation, companionship, and a man leaving and cleaving to his wife to become one flesh. Couples are implored to flee fornication and adultery, as this union models and portrays the true love that God has for His Church.

I endeavoured to highlight some vital points for those who are planning to embark on this lifelong and rewarding journey, as well as those who are already married. Emphasis is placed on three foundational features of this covenant relationship, namely love, trust, and reciprocity (give and take). Each feature is looked at in-depth.

Due consideration is given to the different missiles that have been launched against marriage to destroy it. These are as follows:

a. **Efforts to redefine marriage** against what God intends for it to be, in that marriage is to be between a man and a woman. It is shown in Scriptures that from the foundation of the earth, God performed the first marriage between a man and a woman. This is the example that we should follow.
b. **Adultery and fornication** are dealt with thoroughly, because these are very common fires that marriage is under. This has reached crisis proportions.
c. **Self-centeredness and selfishness** are taking centre stage in many marriages. Spouses are not caring for each other as they should.
d. **The sanctity of marriage** is given great attention and lots of time

is spent on dealing with the threats against it, as well as the restoration and maintenance of this holy estate.

    e. **Sex and intimacy** as designed by God are fully explored. I offer much insight on the restoration of this vital component of marriage.

    f. **Abuses in marriage** could not be overlooked. Abuse is taking place at an alarming rate. This comes in many forms, including physical, verbal, psychological, emotional, financial, and sexual abuse. Each is looked at separately and fully.

    g. **Divorce**—Some of the other fires mentioned here are reduced inclination to procreate, the unprecedented high rate of divorce, women's liberation, and chauvinism.

In order to win the fight for our marriages, we should not stop fighting back, because if we quit, we will never win. It is imperative that I highlight some of the ways in which we should fire back and the necessary tools needed to fight back.

    a. Have the agape or "God type" of love for your spouse
    b. Reintroduce love, trust, and reciprocity
    c. Embrace differences in your spouse
    d. Try not to compete, but to complete each other
    e. Rid your marriage of selfishness

The damages of unforgiveness and its devastating effects on marriage are greatly expounded. Special emphasis is also placed on the root of bitterness and its effects. Attempts are made to highlight some of the major reasons for unforgiveness, including pride, ignorance, lack of trust in other people, and self-reliance, as opposed to trusting God.

I encourage my readers to appreciate, restore, and maintain the sanctity of marriage. Words of caution are also given to men and women who want to be married, are already married, and are soon-to-be married.

CHAPTER 1

THE DEFINITION OF MARRIAGE

We are living in a time when the definition and sanctity of marriage seem to be changing in society, but it remains unchanged in the Word of God. The sanctity of this binding covenant has been seriously desecrated. There is also a cultural distortion of the same. However, marriage is a covenant between a man and a woman. God's Word cannot be made irrelevant. Marriage is the oneness of a man and a woman, whereby the man leaves his parents and cleaves to his wife. In other words, the married couple should be cemented together with permanency. It is meant to be for life. You might call it ancient, if you will, but God is in fact the Ancient of Days, yet His words are from everlasting to everlasting. The definition of marriage does not change, neither with the times nor the seasons.

This is, in fact, a covenant that is divinely instituted by God Himself, from the beginning of creation. Marriage is God's design and is glorious and honourable. It is the act whereby a man and a woman enter this sacred covenant, without reservation. The objective here should be to offer oneself sacrificially in love to his or her spouse. It is also a bond between a man and a woman that is uniquely designed to last for life, except in the case of infidelity, which is sexual unfaithfulness. Marriage is where the hearts, minds, and bodies of the wife and husband are cemented together in a covenant relationship.

Marriage is a special kind of relationship that bears deep parallels between a wedding here on Earth and the relationship that exists between Christ and His Church. Also, it portrays the plan of salvation, whereby we confess Christ as Lord and then accept Him as our Saviour. After this, we become married to Him. Marriage should not be entered into lightly.

Matthew 5:31-32 clearly stipulates that a marriage should only be severed in the case of sexual immorality. Sexual immorality assassinates the very fabric of this holy covenant relationship and totally demonizes its sanctity. It also negatively infringes on the elements of trust and intimacy that form the very backbone of a marriage.

I want to take the time here to highlight some of the features of a marriage covenant. The marriage covenant:
    a. Was designed by God for companionship, procreation, and fulfillment of the agape love of God

b. Involves a man leaving his parents and cleaving or cementing to his wife, becoming one flesh spiritually, emotionally, and physically
c. Is characterized by the agape love of God from a man to his wife
d. Is sacrificial, committed, selfless, and unconditional in nature
e. Involves great caring and sharing
f. Lacks self-centeredness
g. Involves the man occupying a position of headship, but not control and dominance of his wife
h. Involves the woman being in a submissive and supportive role to her own husband, but not that of a doormat
i. Is sanctified by God
j. Is monogamous in nature—lacks polygamy, which has no place in this covenant
k. Prohibits envy and covetousness for another person's spouse
l. Extends throughout one's lifetime (until death)
m. Is divine in nature
n. Is highly sacred
o. Is a covenant and not a contract, although it is ratified by contractual agreements
p. Takes place between a man and a woman by God's design and purpose

Marriage can also be referred to as "the school of marriage," because it bears some similarities to a school. These similarities are listed below for you:

➢ Continuous learning takes place in a school and the same happens in a marriage. In a marriage, learning cannot become redundant.
➢ At times, we are not happy about going to school, but there are benefits to be derived from going, as opposed to not going. Also, in a marriage there are days when you may feel as though you don't want to continue in that union. However, if it was founded on God, I implore you to fight assiduously. Don't give up! It is more beneficial to keep working together for the good of your marriage.
➢ You need to study while in school, so that you will become successful. Likewise, you must fervently study God's Word in your marriage and put them into practice. In school, there is a course outline for each program of study, but in marriage

God's master plan is the outline. Therefore, study and conform to God's master plan for a healthy marriage.
- A school is staffed with teachers or lecturers. There is also a dean or a principal who oversees the smooth running of the school. In the case of a marriage, the Holy Ghost is the teacher, and Christ is the head. Note that if students want to be successful in school, they need to pay keen attention, listen, and follow instructions. This is not different from a marriage; the same policy applies.
- Don't forget that your spouse is symbolic of another student in your class. Neither of you has graduated or has completed your course of study. The bottom line is you are both a work in progress and are both in training.

- Marriage is the only institution of learning where your certificate (Marriage Certificate) is granted to you on the first day of registering. This authenticates you as a student in that school as you prepare for further learning.
- Whenever you are enrolled in school and it is test time, don't leave school and not take the test. Tests are meant to assess you and determine if you are applying the principles learned. This will determine whether you fail or pass. The same applies to the tests you face in a marriage. Don't leave your marriage; instead, prepare yourself for those tests so that you will pass them with flying colours.
- Marriage requires much work, so work collaboratively with your other classmate to complete your assignment.

While there are many similarities between marriage and school, there are also many differences between the two.

- In school, there is an expectation that a graduation will take place at the end of your course of study, but in marriage there isn't. Marriage is meant for continuous learning for life. Don't forget that.
- There are no holidays in marriage. There are no spring breaks. There are no days off or weekends off. There are also no sick days or closures due to inclement weather. Marriage is always in session.
- In marriage, you are not expected to dismiss classes or to drop out. Marriage requires great sacrifice and a high level of commitment to the cause. No absenteeism.

Marriage Covenant versus Contract

Marriage is distinctly different from all other relationships. It is a covenant, not a contract. This covenant is uniquely defined in terms of its unity, the sanctity of this relationship, the intimacy shared, the fellowship, and the mandate to procreate. God is, in fact, the nucleus or the central figure in this covenant.

Let's take the time to look at the definition of a covenant. As defined by the Webster's Dictionary, it is "a mutual agreement between two or more persons." From a biblical standpoint, a marriage covenant is the coming together for lifelong friendship and agreement. This is solemn and binding for life. Whenever a marriage covenant is made, both the man and his wife should solemnly resolve that they will not come apart until death. It carries with it a deep sense of commitment, truth, and responsibility. The word covenant is derived from the Latin term con venire, which means coming together. From a theological perspective, a covenant is also known as berit in the Old Testament era, and it is mainly called a bond. It is also called diaghvkh in the New Testament era. This basically means one person disposing him or herself to another.

Throughout the Scriptures, there are several major covenants mentioned in the Bible, the primary ones are:

1. The Noahic Covenant - Exodus 2:1-33
2. The Abrahamic Covenant - Genesis 12:1-3
3. The Mosaic Covenant - Exodus 2:1-33
4. The Davidic Covenant - 2 Samuel 7:12-16
5. The Covenant of Promise - Jeremiah 31:31-34; Hebrew 8:7-13

Each covenant is ratified by the shedding of blood. In the Old Testament, a covenant was made by the sacrificial slaying of an animal. It was then ratified or validated over the body of the slain animal. The ratification was then done with a procurement and the terms of the covenant. In this procurement, the curse(s) that will come upon the head of the person who violates the covenant was also explained. This solemn process is typological of the curse that would be placed on the violators like the animal that was slain. The covenant had to be sealed with blood.

The marriage covenant is a bond between a man and his wife. It is quite binding in nature and is intended by God to be for life. The marriage covenant is indeed sovereign and transcends the lifetime of a man and his wife.

The vow states, "until death." This means permanency. If broken, except under conditions stipulated in the Scriptures, there are serious consequences.

God intends for couples to enjoy this covenant relationship. Each person is responsible for both fighting for the cause and being absolutely committed to his or her marriage. Forgiveness is one of the major factors in a covenant, and that holds true for marriage as well. In a marriage, there is the daily need to forgive your spouse and release him or her from any wrongs done against you. By doing so, you will not allow bitterness to take root in your marriage.

A covenant is sacrificial. Marriage requires much sacrificial giving of yourself to your spouse for the fulfilment of God's plan. Both of you are expected to be fully committed to this cause. Consistent sacrificial love from God also forms the basis of the covenant, and marriage is by no means an exception. Marriage requires unconditional love for one's spouse for it to be healthy, and should experience much growth; that is the true love that comes from God alone.

Whenever a covenant is established, it should be beneficial to the other party involved, and not for oneself. It should not be done for selfish reasons. Some of the objectives should be to support, love, and care for your spouse, and to offer yourself without reservation for the good and betterment of each other.

Therefore, it is imperative that you see marriage the way God sees it—as a covenant. If your view of marriage is to the contrary, then you won't be able to embrace the permanency of this special type of relationship, neither will you practice and hold dear the unconditional love, sacrifice, and commitment that this covenant carries. Also, you will not be able to hold this covenant relationship in high esteem.

Marriage is so important to God that it mirrors the same type of love and commitment that exists between God (the Bridegroom) and His Church (the bride). We can see throughout Scripture the level of love, care, and commitment that He shows His Church. Due to the nature of this relationship between Jesus and His Church, He paid for it with His own blood. Hence, marriage should not be taken for granted. It is not a simple relationship, but one that is deeply rooted in a covenant. It must be upheld in truth and honesty in the same manner as Christ upholds His Church.

Jesus is quite serious about spiritual adultery between His Church and the world, just like a man would be about his wife. He specifically instructed His people not to have any other gods beside Him. This is both implicit and explicit that you should not have any other spouse, except the one with whom you have made this marriage covenant. Let's not lose sight of the fact that marriage is monogamous in nature. Therefore, there is no room for an extramarital affair. No outsiders should be allowed; they are only out there to derail your marital train. We are not humanly capable of understanding the true meaning of marriage and the mystery of two flesh becoming one, without a divine revelation from God. There must be a spiritual awakening of our understanding.

Here it behooves me to differentiate a contract from a covenant. A contract is an agreement between two or more persons, to do or to not do something. This is for a specific time and place. There is also an offer and an acceptance. Sometimes, there are counter offers. A contract is conditional in nature and is breakable, and the consequences are not as severe as those in a covenant. These consequences are enforceable in the court of law. Whenever contracts are executed, there is an inclination to achieve a desired result. A covenant is an agreement with two, or more, persons. Both parties are responsible to carry out what they have promised to do, or to not do. Certain rights and privileges are also given to those involved. A covenant encompasses a contract but differs in terms of the nature of its contents.

From a legal standpoint, marriage is viewed as a contract with certain rights and responsibilities. However, from a spiritual standpoint, God sees marriage as a covenant relationship. It was designed by God from the beginning of creation. Therefore, His Word takes pre-eminence over man-made laws.

Due to the fact that marriage is a covenant, both you and your spouse should give your best to each other, without reservation. Everything that a marital relationship possesses belongs to both of you. Sharing is a very vital component of this relationship, and your giving should not be contingent on the other person's giving. Marriage is a very special kind of relationship.

CHAPTER 2

THE PURPOSES OF MARRIAGE AS DESIGNED BY GOD

Companionship

From the beginning of creation, when God saw that man was lonely and needed companionship, He created woman. In fact, man needed a helpmate. Although animals were there, the first man Adam was still lonely. That was a sure indication that companionship plays a very important role in marriage. The void that occurs when a man is lonely cannot be filled by anything else in this world—not pets, money, fine cars, or fancy houses.

In fact, there is a natural inclination in a man's heart for a relationship with a woman. According to Maslow's hierarchy of needs, a man yearns to love and be loved. It is a part of his biological make-up and forms the core of one of man's basic needs, after the need for food, clothing, and shelter is satisfied. That is why God's Word declares that a man should leave his mother and father and cleave to his wife. Man's loneliness was not good for him, so God provided the solution by giving him a helpmate.

Becoming One Flesh (Matthew 19:4-5)

If you are not joined to your spouse as one flesh, you will soon dry up and fall off like a broken branch from a tree that has lost its sustenance.

The first marriage was conducted in the Garden of Eden when God gave away the first bride. He gave the woman to the man in marriage, after they were made in His image. This was the only occasion on which God brought the man to the woman. It is, therefore, highly indicative of the fact that this is a special relationship, and second to none, in God's eyes. This clearly indicates that marriage should not be taken lightly. It was designed by God for His glory. In Matthew 19:4-5, Jesus Christ declared that "From the beginning of creation He made them male and female, and for this reason a man shall leave his mother and father and cleave to his wife: and they shall become one flesh." He continued to say, "They are no more twain but one flesh." The process here is that of "twining" but the end and desired result is "one flesh." This clearly shows that God designed marriage by miraculously causing the flesh of two individuals to become one. This is a mystery, and our natural minds cannot comprehend it. We cannot naturally wrap our minds around the possibility of this occurring. Therefore, it is a supernatural act, two hearts becoming as one. Sometimes, both the man and woman in a marriage are from two different geographical locations, ethnicities, cultural backgrounds, and presumably biological connections. However, they are twined into one flesh. Now, this is indeed a masterpiece designed by God. This is the only union whereby this mystery has taken place. One cannot help but say that this is God's doing, and it is a marvellous work amongst us. His hands are most evident in this, and it is for His glory.

The only occasion in the Bible where God commissioned man to leave his parents and cleave and become one flesh is in the case of marriage. This clearly indicates that the bond of marriage is both strong and divine. When you have become one flesh, be faithful to each other.

Men, after you have left your mother and father to cleave to your wife, it is highly recommended that you move from under your parents' chain of command. When you were a child, they were your guides and they directed you in the path that seemed right to them. They were your major decision makers. However, after getting married, your chain of command from your parents must be broken. When you were a child, you spoke and understood as one, now that you have become a man, stop behaving like a child. You have now been placed in a position of headship in your marriage. This is a divine command and responsibility. You are no longer accountable to your parents, and they no longer make major decisions for you and your wife. Neither do they issue instructions to you, as in the past. Don't misinterpret me; they are still your parents and deserve your respect. However, they no longer stand in a position of headship in your life.

Leaving and cleaving applies to you and your wife, not your children. There is a growing trend in marriage where the husband is just sticking around for the children's sake. Men, you were called to cleave to your wife. Had it not been for your wife there would not have been any children. This practice is ungodly and must stop. The bond between you and your spouse is of a different nature from that with your children, and cannot be substituted. That is not God's design.

Sex is meant to be experienced within the context of marriage. It is meant to be quite pleasurable and rewarding. There is glory in virginity. It is sanctified in the sense that your body is kept pure and holy for your spouse. Your body is, therefore, preserved for your partner. Choice vessels or utensils are reserved for special occasions and for special people. A person doesn't take out crystals and china until there is an extra special occasion or a special person to use it. The sanctity that should exist in sex after one gets married is very much connected to abstinence from sex during the pre-marital stage.

Procreation

By God's design, marriage is also intended for the continuation of the human race. From the beginning of time, God instructed the first couple to be "fruitful and multiply." Therefore, a man and his wife are responsible for procreation. This is a mandate from God. Marriage is under intense heat in this area. The missiles are continuously being fired, but don't stop firing back. God's Word takes pre-eminence. He has given honour to His Word, above and beyond His name.

This multiplication process entails the sexual encounter between a man and his wife, resulting in the conceiving and bearing of offspring to replenish the earth. Sex is designed by God to be sacred and to be done only under this covenant condition. It is holy and creates the spiritual and emotional bonding in a marriage. Also, it is the vehicle through which reproduction or procreation takes place. Intimacy in marriage is held in high esteem by God, but is being trampled on in our society.

It is God's intention that the family unit be used to raise up the offspring of a man and his wife. The Scriptures also assure us that children are a blessing from the Lord, so couples who have their quiver filled with children are blessed. Therefore, it is necessary that the family unit be maintained.

Children should be raised in the fear and admonition of the Lord. Parents, it is your responsibility to raise your children right by teaching them Christian morals and principles. They should be taught to respect and conform to God's Word, and also to respect authority. In other words, they should be taught obedience both to God and their parents. Not only should they be taught, but your marriage must exemplify those principles and morals. In addition, they should be taught that their bodies are the temple of God and should not be used as a vessel of immorality. Fornication and adultery are done within one's body. Whoever commits either of them sins against his or her own body.

Prevention of Fornication and Adultery

Marriage is intended to prevent fornication and adultery. It is a biblical instruction that a woman should have her own husband and the same applies to a man having his own wife. The Bible declares that a woman should have her own husband and, if I might add, not somebody else's. When Jesus met the woman of Samaria at the well, she was involved in different adulterous relationships. In case you are not familiar with the story, let me take the time to explain it. Jesus met her at the well and asked her for her husband, and she stated that she had none, and rightly so. The fact is, she had several men that were not her own, and even the one she was living with was not hers. Now, to my female counterparts, if that sounds like you, then you need an encounter with Jesus. After the woman of Samaria had this encounter, she forsook her former lifestyle of being with other women's husbands. She had a complete makeover and became a carrier of the Good News of salvation. Nothing and no one who comes in contact with Jesus remains the same. It is either there is a renewal or total destruction. For example, the woman of Samaria had a renewal, while in the story of Jesus and the fig tree, the tree dried up.

Men, you are not an exemption to this rule. You are prohibited from envying your neighbour's wife. You don't have to covet Uriah's wife, Bathsheba, and lay with her like David. It is advisable that you get your own wife, and when you have done so, stay and operate within your covenant rights. "He who finds a wife, finds a good thing" (Proverbs 18:22).
God has placed in both man and woman the desire to love and be loved, and to be intimate with a member of the opposite sex. This is holy and natural. However, the need for intimacy should be kept within the parameters of marriage.

1 Corinthians 7:5 warns that neither the wife nor the husband should deprive each other of sex; unless there is a mutual agreement to do so. This agreement should be for a limited time only to give oneself over to prayer. Did you hear that? The "limited edition" is the only type that you should employ in your marriage. This warning is given to prevent adultery and other sexual sins. Each spouse has a duty to fulfil each other's needs, and each should endeavour to do so.

In our society, adultery has become the order of the day. This has intercepted the holy covenant of marriage. This is an enemy to the sanctity of marriage, and it is contrary to God's design. Now that you are married, you should not allow adultery to enter your marriage, nor take up residence there. If it has already made its way into this holy covenant, start firing back, and don't stop. Rid your marriage of this foreign body; it is only here to bring death.

Men, don't pursue after and seek satisfaction from the bosom of a strange woman. Seek after your wife and bask in her love. From a biblical standpoint, a strange woman is considered a harlot and a false bride. In other words, drink from your own cistern. You have not made a covenant with her, so don't get entangled with her. A strange woman's lips appear as honeycomb and her mouth is synonymous to that of wormwood. This is, indeed, sharper than a double edged sword. Her words are quite flattering. She is there only to cause shipwreck in your life and to sandbank your relationship with God. Throughout the Bible, strict warnings are given against getting into relationships with strange women. Therefore, keep away from fornication, adultery, and other sexual impurities. The lips of a strange woman seem quite appealing and attractive in the beginning, but in the end they turn out to be sour and bitter as Mara (Proverbs 5:3-4).

In Proverbs 5:18-19, you are instructed to "rejoice in the wife of your youth who is a lovely deer and a graceful doe." Men, you should only find comfort in the breasts of your wife. Ecclesiastes 9:9 also reminds men to find enjoyment in your wife, not in another man or another man's wife. Men, please pay keen attention to what Proverbs 6 has to say to you.

My son, observe the commandment of your father and do not forsake the teaching of your mother; bind them continually on your heart; Tie them around your neck. When you walk about, they will guide you; when you sleep, they will watch over you; And when you awake, they will talk to you. For the commandment is a lamp and the teaching is light; and reproofs for discipline are the way of life to keep you from the evil woman, From the smooth tongue of the adulteress. Do not desire her beauty in your heart, nor let her capture you with her eyelids. For on account of a harlot one is reduced to a loaf of bread, and an adulteress hunts for the precious life. Can a man take fire in his bosom and his clothes not be burned? Or can a man walk on hot coals and his feet not be scorched? So is the one who goes in to his neighbor's wife; whoever touches her will not go unpunished. Men do not despise a thief if he steals to satisfy himself when he is hungry; but when he is found, he must repay sevenfold; he must give all the substance of his house. The one who commits adultery with a woman is lacking sense; he who would destroy himself does it. Wounds and disgrace he will find, and his reproach will not be blotted out. For jealousy enrages a man, and he will not spare in the day of vengeance. He will not accept any ransom, nor will he be satisfied though you give many gifts." (Proverbs 6:20-35)

I want to emphasize that Delilah is dead, but her whoring spirit of deception is still rampant in our society today (Judges 16:22). Therefore, men, be sober and vigilant, because strange women are out there to get you and your marriage. Be careful whose lap you are sleeping in and to whom you are disclosing your marital secrets. If you become joined to them, you will eventually become one flesh with them.

Women, you are not exempt from these warnings. Remember, your bodies are God's temple, so be careful what you allow into your bodies. You are accountable to God in like manner as the men. You are called to be virtuous (Proverbs 31:10-31).

A virtuous woman possesses some distinct qualities. According to Proverbs 31, the virtuous woman:

- Submits herself to the headship of her husband as the head of the household, and she endeavours to understand her husband and to be understood by him
- Is trustworthy and noble
- Takes care of the affairs of her household quite well and is joyful about doing so
- Is productive and is not a time waster
- Is not a busybody in other people's affairs
- Is not slothful in her work
- Applies wisdom with understanding in carrying out her role as a wife
- Patterns the ant by laying up provisions for the winter or in times of need. In other words, she is not wasteful of her resources
- Gives to her neighbours who are in need
- Is a godly and righteous woman who eschews evil
- Is very discreet
- Governs her tongue well, with wisdom
- Gives good and godly advice to others where necessary, especially to those in her household
- Fears and reverences God
- Is a blessing to her family and brings respect to her husband while among others
- Respects and honours her husband
- Represents the Church. Therefore, she is a good portrayal of the bride
- Has great value
- Employs wisdom in the acquisition of properties for her family
- Carries herself with dignity and gets respect from others, and also extends respect to others
- Is not a brawler
- Receives praise from her husband and children
- Displays great strength by standing firm in times of adversity

In the Bible, Ruth is a perfect example of a virtuous woman. She is the only woman in the bible that is referred to with this title.

Women, did you know that in Proverbs 22:1 it is said that "A good name is rather to be chosen than great riches and loving favour rather than silver and gold"? This speaks volumes. It is quite clear that you should strive to possess a good name.

"In the same way, you wives, be submissive to your own husbands [subordinate, not as inferior, but out of respect for the responsibilities entrusted to husbands and their accountability to God, and so partnering with them] so that even if some do not obey the word [of God], they may be won over [to Christ] without discussion by the godly lives of their wives, when they see your modest and respectful behaviour [together with your devotion and appreciation—love your husband, encourage him, and enjoy him as a blessing from God]. Your adornment must not be merely external—with interweaving and elaborate knotting of the hair, and wearing gold jewelry, or [being superficially preoccupied with] dressing in expensive clothes; but let it be [the inner beauty of] the hidden person of the heart, with the imperishable quality and unfading charm of a gentle and peaceful spirit, [one that is calm and self-controlled, not overanxious, but serene and spiritually mature] which is very precious in the sight of God. For in this way in former times the holy women, who hoped in God, used to adorn themselves, being submissive to their own husbands and adapting themselves to them; just as Sarah obeyed Abraham [following him and having regard for him as head of their house], calling him lord. And you have become her daughters if you do what is right without being frightened by any fear [that is, being respectful toward your husband but not giving in to intimidation, nor allowing yourself to be led into sin, nor to be harmed]." (1 Peter 3:1-7 AMP)

Taking the Lifelong Journey of Marriage

Love

Godly wisdom and much prayer are important when entering into the ordinance of marriage. This relationship is deeply rooted in love and commitment. It is very binding in nature and should last until death, except in the case of unfaithfulness in the form of abandonment and adultery. Therefore, it should not be torn apart for frivolous reasons. Taking the actual marital journey involves having agape love. This is the kind of love that only God can enable you to develop. It is unconditional, selfless, sacrificial, and very spiritual.

Men are commissioned to love their wives as Christ loves the Church, to the extent that He gave His life for it. Don't be mistaken, I am not implying that you give your life for your wife. This analogy is used to show the extent to which a man should love his wife. The Bible is clear that all others should be left behind after you get married. This circle of marriage is only made of two halves—you and your wife.

As a wife, you are commissioned to submit yourself to your husband. This is mutual and of vital importance. A marriage without love cannot withstand the test of time. Love in your marriage will enable you to weather the storms of life and the contrary winds that will blow against you. Wives are also expected not to bring any foreign bodies into the marriage. It is holy, so keep it clean. Not only is it clean, but it is also honourable, so don't dishonour it.

Trust
This is highly foundational for a marriage. A marriage without trust is like building a house without the necessary building blocks to anchor it properly into the ground. Two cannot walk and live in agreement and unity if the element of trust is missing.
Trust can be defined as the ability to prove something or someone to be reliable, after critical assessment. This is done upon close evaluation and observation to identify and establish quality. From a biblical perspective, trust means to have faith or total confidence in someone, based on integrity, honesty, and truth.

Reciprocity
This is the give and take component of marriage. It can also be called forgiveness. Reciprocity is not conditional in nature, and should be practiced daily in your marriage. Reciprocity is deeply rooted in grace and mercy. This should be given even if it seems like your spouse doesn't deserve it. Don't forget that each day of your life you stand in need of grace and mercy, so be willing to extend it. There are great benefits to be derived from such a healthy and godly practice.
 You should learn to give and take in your marriage. Each person is an individual. Therefore, each has his or her individual differences and characteristics. Remember, neither of you is able, or was given the responsibility, to transform the other; that is God's job.

Acknowledge Who Is the Head of the Marriage
The man is the head of his wife by God's appointment. It is synonymous to Christ being the head of the Church. Men, you are expected to not be abusive or domineering; instead, you should comfort and shower her

with your love. You are also expected to protect her from harm and danger. If you are demonstrating characteristics to the contrary, then you are abusing your headship as designed by God.

Men, as the head, you are encouraged to function from a position of wisdom, knowledge, and understanding in your marriage. By so doing, you must show her affection and comfort. It is also your responsibility to provide for your household. Don't fall into the category of infidels.

God should be the foundation and the central force in your marriage. He is the rock and firm foundation. Marriage is like a house. If a house is built on sand, it is easily blown down by light wind, rain, or the simplest of storms. Be wise and build your marriage on God's foundation. You won't regret it. Allowing God to take centre stage in your marriage takes supernatural intervention. Although the husband serves from a position of headship, God should be the Lord of your marriage. He should be sought for directions and guidance in whatever you do in this union. He is your source, not your spouse nor your job. Exalt Him as such.

Endeavour to desist from relying on your own understanding; you will fail. Allow the wisdom of God to have its full course in your marriage. Wisdom should be a principal feature that is highly functional in this union. However, you should also make every effort to get understanding. Wisdom, knowledge, and understanding work in collaboration with each other (Proverbs 4:7).

CHAPTER 3

THE MISSILES AGAINST MARRIAGE

The missiles against marriage must not be taken lightly. There is a demonic attack to destroy your seed and to break down the family unit. Fire, as defined by the Encyclopedia Britannica 2015, is "the rapid burning of combustible material, with the evolution of heat, and is usually accompanied by heat." From a weaponry perspective, it also carries the meaning of discharging a gun at your enemies. Fire can be verbal as well as physical.

Fire moves at a rapid speed as oxidization takes place. As oxygen and fuel are combined, flames are produced. However, extremely high temperatures are necessary for the advancement of flames. To be "under fire" means that one is being attacked or is being encamped by the enemy. This phrase also means to undergo a test that is quite intense, a fiery trial. A trial of torment from one's enemy involves intense repeated attacks being launched, which can also come in the form of criticisms. Being "under fire" can also include the discharging of bullets, missiles, rockets, and other projectiles from one's enemy.

The sacred union of marriage is under heavy attack. The enemy is encamping around this covenant to destroy it as well as the family unit in which it operates. Projectiles are being launched from the enemy's fierce weapons against this sacred union, daily. Marriage is being put through severe tests, repeatedly. These tests are symbolic of the discharging of bullets and missiles. The objective is to destroy the very foundation of marriage. Be reminded that anything that has its foundation built by God and that remains in God cannot be destroyed. God places a high level of honour on marriage and will not stand back and watch lawmakers and other people of influence in our society dishonour it. God also honours the family, and anyone who tries to destroy it will be accountable to Almighty God.

Couples are spending less and less time with their families due to long hours at work in order to service high debts and stay above the poverty level. This has greatly contributed to the breakdown in the family unit. A majority of the problems that we are currently facing are due to the breakdown of the family unit. Whenever this happens, the children suffer and are torn apart, emotionally, physically, and otherwise. Some have become victims of suicide, depression, and teenage pregnancy, among other things. There are some who have turned to drugs and alcohol abuse as the solution to their problems, placing themselves in a worse position.

The breakdown of the family unit has led to many children being raised by a single parent or by foster parents. This has caused more grief, hardship, pain, and frustration on both the remaining parent and the children. The rate of divorce has also skyrocketed, resulting in severe pain, and hardship on an emotional, financial, and spiritual level.

Now, there is another fire that is plaguing marriage and that is the breakdown of marriage that has not resulted in a divorce, but rather in a legal or judicial separation. Some couples are not legally divorced but have chosen to do this type of separation. They are legally released from the obligation to live together. The bottom line is that the very fabric of the marriage has suffered decay. This is not a part of God's plan for marriage.

Some of the contributing factors that lead to legal or judicial separation are adultery and desertion of one spouse by the other. There are also cases where both parties have come to an agreement to be legally separated. Some have done a separation of convenience in order to qualify for and secure social benefits. Some families have benefitted more from being a sole support unit than a couple. These incentives have led many families to break up voluntarily or involuntarily.

There is a moral decay in the fabric of marriage. Immorality is at an all-time high and continues to rise at an alarming rate. In addition, relativism has taken pre-eminence over the Word of God, but God's principles and Word should be seen as the only absolute. His Word is from everlasting to everlasting. His name is highly exalted, yet He esteemed His Word above His name.

Some of the fires against marriage are dealt with in detail below.

Fire #1
Efforts to Redefine Marriage

There has been a concerted effort to change the true meaning of marriage and replace it with man-made laws. Let us not lose sight of the fact that God doesn't change, and His Word stands forever. From the beginning, after God created everything, He saw that man was lonely and needed companionship. God saw that it was not good for man to be alone, so he made Eve from the bone that came out of Adam's side. He made a woman to satisfy man's need for companionship.

Fire#2
Adultery

The sacred union of marriage is being plagued by adultery. Its sanctity is being trampled on by those who were supposed to hold it in high esteem.

This is like a rose that is being trampled on the ground. Unfaithfulness to one's partner is in high fashion, and many are wearing it with pride. When you are unfaithful in your marriage, you are being unfaithful to God Himself.

Job 31:1 says, "I have made covenant with my eyes; how then can I gaze upon a virgin?" Here, Job saw that it was important for his eyes not to lead him away in the wrong direction when he sees a woman. He made a solemn resolution that he would not look at a female that is not his wife in an inappropriate manner. He wanted to stay pure, even in his thoughts.

Proverbs 6:27-29 says, "Can a man take fire to his bosom, and his clothes not be burned? Can one walk on hot coals, and his feet not be seared? So is he who goes in to his neighbor's wife; whoever touches her shall not be innocent."

Fire # 3
The Lack of True Sacrificial Love for One's Spouse
Love is kind and keeps no record of wrongs. It allows you to look beyond your spouse's faults, and see them the way God sees them. It does not repay evil for evil, but good for evil. Therefore, desist from keeping records—both physically and mentally—of the errors and even the wrongs done by your spouse in your marriage. If you keep records, then the sun will go down while you are still angry with each other, and this should not be the case. Love is also sacrificial, so give of yourself unselfishly to your spouse.

Fire# 4
Selfishness and Self-Centeredness
Selfishness has currently taken centre stage in marriage, instead of God. He is supposed to be central in this covenant, not you. The love of God has gotten cold in marriage, and now it is each one for himself or herself. Marriage is experiencing a serious division between husbands and wives. The motto seems to be "It's all about me." On most occasions, wives are no longer submissive to their husbands, and husbands are no longer loving and caring for their wives, as instructed in the Bible.

Fire# 5
Reduced Inclination to Procreate
Procreation, a mandate from God, is being greatly challenged with the desperate attempts to redefine marriage. Now, it only takes a man and a woman to come together to be fruitful and multiply.
The quest to be at the top of one's career and the acquisition of more wealth,

fame, and fortune is also firing on marriage. This quest is affecting marriage in a negative way, in that the mandate to multiply and replenish the earth is not the focal point in many marriages. Couples are putting off having children to concentrate on their career. There are some people who have gotten married with different value systems in regards to procreation. As a result of the reduced inclination to procreate, it has become quite trendy for other things to be embraced as offspring.

Fire # 6
Failure to Become One Flesh

Some men are failing to leave mother and father and be joined to their wives only. They have physically left their father and mother, but are still joined to them from a commander's point of view. They are still under the headship of their parents and they do not stand up and take responsibility in their own marriage. They do not cleave to their wives because they have not left mother and father as the Bible instructed them to do. As a result, any major decision to be made in their marriage, in collaboration with their wives, is made and sanctioned by their parents. This is indeed a dangerous weapon in marriages.

I do not want these statements to be misconstrued that once you are married you should abandon your parents or their advice. Their advice can be very helpful, but they should no longer be the central advisors in your marriage. Once married, you have now come into this union to which you are called to take up a headship position, but not with any iota of dominance over your wife. Always remember that you and your wife should work together as a team for one common goal—to bring glory to God. You are no longer "mama's little boy," you have now grown into an adult.

Some men are also failing to leave others behind and cleave to their wives. Many are joined to the earthly possessions of their wives, instead of their wives. Some of these things may include her bank account, house, car, or opportunities. Many are only drawn to their wives due to her facial beauty and physique. However, these physical features may change, sometimes due to childbirth, sickness, ageing, or due to an accident.

On the other hand, although they have physically left their parents' home, many women are still tied to it, emotionally. Some are still allowing their parents to negatively advise them on what they should do in their marriage. Married women, you are no longer "Daddy's little girl." You are in a covenant relationship with your husband, which means you have certain covenant rights and responsibilities. You are no longer supposed to allow your parents to make major decisions for your life and your marriage.

Instead, you should work in conjunction with your husband as a team. Women, you are also expected to be one with your husband after he has left his mother and father and is cleaving to you. Don't try to become attached with another; God will not put His stamp of approval on that, because that clearly defines an extramarital affair.

Also, some women are only drawn to their husband's earthly possessions and physical attributes. Whenever this happens, it creates serious problems in the marriage, and eventually ends in divorce.

Fire # 7
Pornography

Pornography and other sexual fantasies should not replace your commitment to be faithful in your marriage. One must endeavour to guard what you watch because the eye is the medium through which one is enticed, then tempted, and finally drawn away into lust. The eye is the first point of entry into your mind. Even if you have not physically participated in the act of adultery or fornication, the fact that you have lusted after it means you have sinned and you are, therefore, guilty (Matthew 5:28). Flee fornication and allow your body to be a vessel of honour. Let holiness abound in you and flow freely.

In addition, pornography via social media has created some wild and unrealistic desires and expectations in marriages. Some of these desires and expectations cannot normally be fulfilled by one's spouse. Whenever this happens, dissatisfaction, frustration, and conflict will arise, causing the unsatisfied spouse to start looking outside of the covenant relationship for sexual gratification. In some cases, this has resulted in divorce. Desist from imposing these unrealistic sexual expectations on your spouse! Remember, your body is the temple of God; don't desecrate it.

Fire # 8
Alarmingly High Divorce Rate

Globally, the rate of divorce has skyrocketed. Just look at the statistics. The rate of divorce is at an all-time high, especially in Christendom. The divorce rate in the Church is almost on par with that of the world. In his paper, "How common is divorce and what are the reasons?" noted marriage scholar and therapist Dr. William H. Doherty gave an alarming overview of the rate of divorce in the US as well as some given reasons. He says, "In the United States, researchers have estimated that 40%–50% of all first marriages, and 60% of second marriages, will end in divorce." A recent national survey found that the most common reason given for divorce was "lack of commitment" (73% said this was a major reason). Other significant reasons included too much arguing (56%), infidelity (55%), marrying too young (46%), unrealistic expectations (45%), lack of equality in the relationship (44%), lack of preparation for marriage (41%), and abuse (29%). People often give more than one reason, so the percentages add up to more than 100% .

Lack of commitment comes in the form of unwillingness to commit to the marriage sexually, and to the sacrifices that are necessary for a good marriage.

Infidelity is indeed amongst the top reasons for divorce. This has taken place and still continues to take place at an alarming rate. Unfortunately, this is also quite frequent amongst people of faith.

Lack of equality in the relationship comes in various forms, including difference in value systems, cultural differences, and differences in interests. Cultural differences have contributed to divorce, in that many people have gotten married to partners from different cultural backgrounds, without conducting proper research into each other's culture. In other words, they have not taken the time to educate themselves on the traditions, customs, religious practices, and even the food of their partner. After getting married, they realize that this disparity in their cultures is so major that conflicts arise and eventually result in a marital breakdown and ultimately divorce.

Differences in value systems continue to contribute to the rate of divorce. When each spouse places different values on important matters, it affects the marriage. These values, on most occasions, are at the opposite sides of the spectrum. Whenever this is the case, and each is not willing to respect the other's views, disagreements and conflicts will arise.

Abuse has also caused many divorces. Abuse comes in many forms, namely drugs and alcohol, physical abuse, financial abuse, and emotional abuse. Drugs and alcohol abuse can cause the user to become incoherent and irrational at times. They are not able to contribute to the marriage in a meaningful way, thus creating a strain on the other party and the marriage. Sometimes, drug and alcohol abuse robs the marriage of needed finances. This then creates a negative chain reaction on the union. Also, at times the drug-abusing spouse becomes physically and emotionally abusive to the other spouse and other members of the family unit.

Marriage is undergoing intense heat, but don't stop firing back. If you are in a God-ordained marriage covenant today and there are many attacks being launched against you, I implore you to fire back at those things that

[1] http://www.divorce.usu.edu/files/uploads/Lesson3.pdf

are warring against your marriage. I am not making reference to those who have entered marriage wrongly. There is a right and wrong way to enter marriage. There are those who have walked down the aisle together in a ceremony, but it was not orchestrated by God, so they truly have no business being together. In fact, they had a ceremony, not a covenant; for example, those who have intercepted or ambushed other unions and have become thieves. Scripture specifies that if you have not entered by the door, then you are a thief and a robber (John 10:1). You have come only to steal, kill, and destroy a covenant relationship. Your reason for doing this is diabolic, and you were not sent from God. It is envy and covetousness that have entered your heart. The Bible specifically states, "You shall not covet your neighbour's wife" (Exodus 20:17). God is not in the least pleased with this type of behaviour, and He does not bless the sin committed. If that is you, then repent and turn away from your sin.

God meant marriage to be for life. It should only be put asunder due to sexual unfaithfulness. "What God has joined together, let no man put asunder," (Matthew 19:6). Fire back with all that is within you and with God's empowerment. Love, trust, and reciprocity should be the foundation of your union. With God as the head, this union shall withstand the test of time. Marriage should not be taken lightly, nor should it be entered into haphazardly. Moreover, one should not put their partner away for frivolous reasons. Biblically, God allows divorce only on the grounds of adultery. The bottom line is He hates divorce.

Men, stop abandoning the wives of your youth and remarrying strange women and women of strange gods. Malachi 2:14 specifically tells us that God cut off a whole nation for doing this. The wife of your youth is meant to be your companion for life. God is a witness in this case and clearly warns you in Malachi 2:14 to pay keen attention to your spirit and not to deal treacherously with your wife. Don't put her away, unless on the grounds of sexual unfaithfulness that is not repented of. In verse Malachi 2:16, it says, "He hates putting away." If you do put away your wife, then you are compared to "one that covers violence." That is heavy stuff.

The "wife of your youth" is the woman that is supposed to be your lifelong companion. You should have your strongest emotional ties with this woman. Also, she should be the one with whom you have shared everything, including your dearest secrets, love, joy, and pain. Most importantly, you should share your most intimate moments physically. Marriage is monogamous in nature, and should not include an alien or aliens. People are entering into marriage for wrong reasons. Some do so for financial security, outside pressures from friends and family, immigration purposes, and other basic opportunities that can be derived from doing so. In other words, a significant number of people have gotten married without being in a state of readiness. Due to being unprepared, many marriages are unable to withstand the pressures of the inevitable storms of life.

Fire #9
Abuse in Marriage

Abuse, specifically child abuse, has very destructive effects on its victims, which often run throughout the lifetime of the victim. Victims of abuse tend to believe that they are at fault; this has devastating effects, as it robs them of their dignity and self-worth. It also dehumanizes and demoralizes them, causing them to feel worthless and deserving of this malicious and evil act. Most victims are caught in an emotional prison, practically being issued a life sentence, and held in a position where they cannot arise easily to explore and maximize their true potential.

It is mostly true that some souls are mangled for a lifetime and attract predators for life. The effects of abuse are deep-rooted, and they cripple the victims. Abuse retards or disables the developmental process of a child, and permanently inflicts internal scars. These scars manifest themselves externally in many ways. Many victims, in turn, go in pursuit of partners with the characteristics of their abuser. Research has supported that observation. This is a recurring cycle. Once molested or raped, the probability that it will be repeated is true in many cases. However, there are exceptions, because there are many cases where after a person has been raped, they get therapeutic help and have overcome the effects of this abuse. Combined with divine intervention, they now see themselves the way God sees them and discover their true self-worth. They then realize that God has a better plan for their lives. Whenever that happens, they are also able to see themselves as faultless for the abuse that took place. They are able to see the abuser as demonic and one who is on a diabolic assignment from Satan. There are also cases where after the victims become more aware of the tricks of the predators, they show much resilience and exhibit reasonable cognitive functions, remarkable growth, renewed strength, and tenacity.

In the case of children, if abuse takes place during the period of their most formative years—which are crucial to self-development—and is left untreated, it will negatively affect their adolescent stage. During the adolescent stage, teenagers frantically try to develop an identity by trial and error. Regrettably, this causes many people to walk around with a distorted concept of who they really are. People in their sphere of influence have also contributed to this distortion. Many people are dysfunctional in their adult years and have not maximized their true potential due to messages conveyed to them in this manner. Sadly, they have believed it and accepted it as their portion. No one has the right to define your identity. Your true identity is found in God. Parents need to be vigilant about the message communicated to their children, even in our schools. There is lots of abuse taking place in our schools today.

Fire # 10
Reduced Inclination to Marry

People are now choosing to cohabitate as opposed to embracing the marriage covenant. They are doing this for several reasons. Some do it for convenience, or as an opportunity to get where they want to get to in life. Others are doing it for fear of the responsibilities of a commitment. They don't wish to be committed to a spouse; instead, they wish to stay casual. Selfishness and self-centeredness are also among the major reasons why some people are not inclined to get married. This is not God's will for your life. He performed the first marriage in the Garden of Eden with Adam and Eve. He did not use an animal or pet to solve man's problem of loneliness.

Fire # 11
Financial Matters

This is another missile that is being fired at marriage, daily. Marriages are experiencing lots of problems in this area. This has caused a break down in the family unit, causing separation and ultimately divorce. Therefore, ensure that both you and your spouse are in unity regarding your finances. Some might consider this trivial to their marriage, but being unified in your finances is critical to a successful marriage.

Fire # 12
Woman's Liberation (feminism)

Women are considering themselves liberated to the extent that they are controlling and obnoxious to their husbands, as opposed to being supportive. I just want to clarify here that I am not implying that women must be victims of inequality in relation to their spouses, neither are they to be trampled on by their husbands. Husbands and wives are meant to complement each other. However, women's liberation is taken to a level whereby some women are even refusing to marry, because they see themselves as being highly independent without a husband. This is especially happening in cases where these women are positioned highly on the social, economic, and financial ladder.

Fire # 13
Chauvinism

Some men tend not to stand in a position of headship as they ought to. Instead, they stand in a position of lordship, exercising rigid control and dominance over their wives. Men, you are not superior to your wives in God's eyes. You are both equal before Him. If that is occupying your thoughts, attitudes, and behaviour, then this is a lie from the pit of hell. She is indeed your help mate. Ephesians 5:25-33 (AMP) says:

"Husbands, love your wives [seek the highest good for her and surround her with a caring, unselfish love], just as Christ also loved the church and gave Himself up for her, so that He might sanctify the church, having cleansed her by the washing of water with the word [of God], so that [in turn] He might present the church to Himself in glorious splendor, without spot or wrinkle or any such thing; but that she would be holy [set apart for God] and blameless. Even so husbands should and are morally obligated to love their own wives as [being in a sense] their own bodies. He who loves his own wife loves himself. For no one ever hated his own body, but [instead] he nourishes and protects and cherishes it, just as Christ does the church, because we are members (parts) of His body. FOR THIS REASON A MAN SHALL LEAVE HIS FATHER AND HIS MOTHER AND SHALL BE JOINED [and be faithfully devoted] TO HIS WIFE, AND THE TWO SHALL BECOME ONE FLESH. This mystery [of two becoming one] is great; but I am speaking with reference to [the relationship of] Christ and the church. However, each man among you [without exception] is to love his wife as his very own self [with behaviour worthy of respect and esteem, always seeking the best for her with an attitude of loving-kindness], and the wife [must see to it] that she respects and delights in her husband [that she notices him and prefers him and treats him with loving concern, treasuring him, honouring him, and holding him dear]."

In summary, the fires are many and they appear in different forms. To reiterate, here is an itemized list of some of the fires marriage is under:
- Changing the role of gender in marriage from what God intended
- Redefinition of marriage
- Increased inclination to cohabitate as man and wife, without entering into the covenant relationship of marriage
- High rate of sexual immorality
- Putting away a marriage for frivolous reasons, without the grounds of sexual unfaithfulness
- Lack of permanency in the duration of this union

CHAPTER 4

WAYS TO KEEP FIRING BACK TO WIN THE FIGHT FOR THE PRESERVATION OF MARRIAGE

It is very important that we don't stop firing back in response to the missiles that are being directed at marriage. We cannot lose the fight. The family unit is to be maintained because this is where society and generations to come are going to benefit the most. Let's leave a good legacy for generations to inherit. A broken family is symbolic of a city whose fence is broken down and everything is running wild, in and out of it. Children often start to run wild when this deterioration happens in the family.

God is very much interested in the preservation of the family. "Children are an heritage of the Lord" (Psalm 127:3). You are considered especially blessed when your quiver is full of them. Don't take this for granted. This is also an awesome and an honourable responsibility. Children are to be raised in the fear of God; this will enable them to honour you as parents. This has a chain effect.

I am convinced that the most important way that we can fire back is to seek the face of God for direction before we enter this covenant of marriage, and remain there constantly thereafter. The process of leaving and cleaving is not humanly possible by ourselves; we need God's intervention. We need to return to God's definition and design for marriage. Let us all work assiduously to reform our morals and values concerning marriage and esteem it highly. Spend time in prayer for marriages and may the spiritual eyes of your understanding be awakened.

I want to take the time to identify some of the ways in which we can fight back for the institution of marriage. I hope you will find these points helpful and rewarding.

GET RID OF SELFISHNESS AND SELF-CENTEREDNESS IN MARRIAGE

Men, you are meant to be the head of your wives, but not by abusing her. Instead, care for her and provide for your household; don't be worse than an infidel (1 Timothy 5:8). The marriage covenant is about sharing your lives with each other for the glory of God. After you become one in flesh, selfishness should have no part in your union. When you are selfless, you tend to put your spouse's needs ahead of yours.

Women, you ought to be submissive to your own husband, not someone else's. You have been twined with the flesh of your husband. However, you are not a doormat, rather you have become one.

It is important that you show your gratitude for your spouse and not talk down to your spouse. Talk with your spouse, and not at him or her. Marriage involves denial of oneself on a daily basis. Be mindful of your spouse and his or her feelings. This will go a long way in your marriage. Remember to not direct unkind words towards your spouse. Words of this nature can be very harmful to your spouse and to your marriage. I want to defy the myth that "sticks and stones can break your bones but words can never hurt you." Let's rearrange our thinking, negative words can break one's spirit badly, if not corrected. Especially in the case where these negative words were uttered by someone of influence or significance in your life. Negative words can, in fact, scar you for life.

This negative type of behaviour has no place in marriage, because you are required to share with your spouse prayerfully, sexually, and emotionally. This includes giving of yourself to each other for mutual fulfillment, which plays a big role in becoming one. In addition, this also means sharing all your possessions with your spouse.

DEVELOP AND MAINTAIN THE AGAPE LOVE FOR YOUR SPOUSE

Marriage is also under the fire of lack of love, trust, and reciprocity for one's spouse. Love is intended to be the nucleus or the central part of a marriage, but has been replaced by lust and infatuation for others. There are four kinds of love, namely agape, eros, philia, and storge. You should allow the agape love to grow and take residence in your union. Love each other unconditionally, sacrificially, and selflessly. God gave the woman to the man as a precious gift from the beginning of time, in the Garden of Eden. She was also handcrafted. Wow! What a priceless masterpiece! The Scriptures state that "He who finds a wife finds a good thing" (Proverbs 18:22). Upon this premise, stop taking each other for granted, if you are guilty of such act.

Agape love is the sacrificial love that is not based on any conditions. It allows you to give of yourself selflessly to your spouse, and it lacks self-centeredness. Jesus portrays this type of love for His Father and to all humanity. This type of love enables one to give of oneself without reservation, even if it is unmerited. This is the highest form of love.

Eros is the kind of love that is sexually passionate and is displayed greatly during intimacy. The Book of Solomon demonstrates this quite well.

This type of love exists between a man and his wife. It creates a natural sexual desire for one's spouse. Physical attraction is one of its characteristics. Philia love is a brotherly type of love that allows one to show affection during friendship. It enables one to form friendships with others and to show care and compassion. This is the type of love that people of God show for each other.

Storge love is very natural and occurs between parents, children, siblings, and other relatives. It is the family type of love that causes families to be closely knitted.

Men, you are commissioned by God to love your wives as God loves His Church. That is indeed a very deep kind of love. You are to love your wives as yourselves. This type of love is quite peculiar and highly affectionate in nature. This love is unconditional and sacrificial. It is not dependent on her vital statistics, as these will change as the years go by. Neither is it dependent on her earthly possessions. Remember that this love is supposed to be unconditional. Your love should not change when an alien or strange woman comes along. You are in covenant with your wife. Gold is not the only thing that glitters; counterfeits do also and even more than gold.

Women, you are also expected to render due benevolence to your spouse, and not to another. This is by God's design, and you are in a covenant with your spouse. Love for him should not be dependent on the car he drives, the house on the hillside, nor the lavish vacations. The size of his bank account should not be the binding factor between you and him.

God also requires that you submit yourself to your own husband, in the Lord. This includes honouring and obeying him, in the things that are right, that is. This should also be done with humility, sincerity, and fidelity. It is extremely important that you become aware of the fact that adultery does not only take place physically, but also in your thoughts. I implore you, therefore, that you guard your thoughts. Whatever you formulate in your thoughts you will eventually act upon, if you don't take control. Men, if you look upon a woman who is not your wife and lust after her, you have already committed a sinful act. This goes also for my female counterparts. Stop fantasizing about having a sexual encounter with a man who is not your spouse. It is devilish.

RESTORATION & MAINTENANCE OF TRUST & RECIPROCITY
TRUST

Allow trust to take its free course in your marriage. This is of vital importance to your covenant. Live your lives unquestionably. Don't allow your good to be evil spoken of. Remember to be transparent with your spouse, so there will not be any reason to mistrust each other. Also, your words should be your bond, knowing that all liars will have a spot in the lake of fire on judgement day.

Trust that is supposed to be in a marriage has become a tottering fence. In other words, it has broken down, or is breaking down, in some cases. It is being replaced by prenuptial agreements. There is supposed to be transparency between both spouses, but unfortunately it is lacking for the most part. Truth that is meant to be within your inward parts is terribly lacking, and lies and deception have taken a stronghold.

Allow your words to be your bond. Let your yes be yes and your no be no. A covenant should not be taken lightly. The vows that you made at your marriage ceremony are meant to be unbreakable, except in the case of infidelity. You have vowed to "Forsake all others" and to cleave to your spouse. The phrase "all others" includes all extramarital affairs.

Trust in marriage is necessary for a couple to be able to freely express themselves and be open with each other. Each person in a marriage should be able to feel secure in this covenant. The presence of trust enables both of you to feel connected to your spouse as your soul mate—one who not only loves you physically but loves you down to your soul. Trust is indeed one of the major building blocks on which marriage is built. It adds strength to your marriage and to any other type of relationship.

Remember, trust is not innate, and because of this you must prove yourself trustworthy before trust can be ascribed to you. Don't be mistaken, it is earned. This also holds true for your spouse. Allow honesty, truthfulness, and integrity to be a part of you. Gird your loins with them. There should be a high level of trust in your marriage, so that you will be free and comfortable to disclose your innermost thoughts to your spouse, with the assurance that this will not be used against you or be shared with others.

Trust is necessary for transparency and vice versa. Whenever you are honest with each other in your marriage, trust will be further developed. Where there is trust in your marriage, it will allow both of you to remove the masks that might be present. You cannot truly trust someone that you don't really know, so take the time to know each other well. It is worth it. Whenever there is trust built into your marriage, it provides security, knowing that this person to whom you are married will be faithful to you, even in the darkest night or in your absence. Both of you will be able to relax, emotionally. Trust forms a part of the cornerstone in a marriage. Therefore, it is greatly advised that you endeavour to have trust in your relationship. To build trust, each of you should be honest and transparent with each other from the premarital stage. There should be no grey areas in your relationship from the beginning. If there is, then take the necessary time to correct that, especially if found before getting married.

Regarding financial matters in your marriage, you should be very transparent, as in other areas. This is a very sensitive area, and both of you should be conscious of this. Lack of trust relating to financial matters has resulted in many separations, breakups, and divorces. Therefore, be watchful for this. You should have confidence in each other and trust one another. You should prove yourself to be trustworthy, and vice versa. Strive to be a person of integrity and good character. Throughout the duration of your marriage, you should forgive your spouse and be forgiven of your spouse for hurting him or her. At times, there may even be matters that you consider to be simple, but they cause hurt to your spouse, so don't take things for granted.

There has to be willingness on the part of both of you, after forgiveness is granted or accepted, to desist from engaging in the same type of behaviour that caused the hurt in the first place. For example, if there happens to be an ex-spouse that is maintaining very close contact with you, that person can be emotionally damaging to your current spouse. A word of wisdom here, please pay close attention to it. The word ex-spouse, as defined by the Cambridge Advanced Learner's Dictionary, "is someone who was once a wife, husband, or partner in the past." It is highly suggestive that your ex-spouse should be history and not be a part of your current marriage. Being too close to such a person can cause insecurity and lack of trust to develop in one's spouse. This close connection to one's ex-spouse can result in unfaithfulness to your current spouse. Let your ex remain your ex, and don't bring him or her into your current season. This is a new season that has begun in your life; embrace it as such. In the Book of Exodus, the Children of Israel departed from Egypt in haste and in great numbers. They did not remain with their enemies after God delivered them. There are valuable lessons to be learned from this.

If you, or your spouse, have suffered brokenness and deception in the past due to broken relationships or marriages, the development of trust in your current marriage may be even more difficult than in your past. In this case, ensure that you start out building trust in your current marriage properly by being honest. Honesty is certainly the best of policies; practice it daily. Let truth be dominant in your inward parts. Express yourself openly to your spouse. Be patient as you communicate with your spouse. True intimacy and oneness in a marriage cannot be properly achieved without trust and honesty. It is also important that you clear the air, so to speak, of any matter that might cause ill-feelings or guilt. Both of you need to communicate about this. If this guilt is due to any deceptive activities on your part, then you need to bring it before God and confess it. Ask Him to shine His light into this dark area of your life and illuminate the darkness. You also need to seek forgiveness from your spouse and be willing to receive it from him or her, when granted. Too many people still walk around with feelings of guilt, even when God and others have forgiven them.

After trust is broken down, it needs to be rebuilt. The rebuilding of trust can be a very painful and devastating process in a marriage. It requires twice as much patience, love, and time than it took in the first place. Therefore, it is important that you stand on guard for the trust in your marriage. Do not allow it to be eroded by dishonesty and falsehood. Be transparent as much as possible, with wisdom. Guard the gates of trust and don't let anyone or anything remove this vital building block from the foundation of your marriage.

Here is a list of helpful suggestions regarding the rebuilding of trust:
- Be purposeful about rebuilding trust in your marriage, and strive for it with truth
- Try to discover the severity of the mistrust and work on it
- Strategize the route that both of you will take to achieve the restoration of trust in your marriage
- Let justice prevail throughout the whole process
- Both of you should be determined that you will learn from past mistakes and work assiduously against any such action becoming repetitive
- Give truth full access and allow it to be very active in your marriage. This will not happen overnight, so this needs to be properly nurtured with time and patience.
- Much forgiveness must be given and received with deep love
- Stop the blaming game and work together in this rebuilding process
- Allow your words to be your bond. Let your yes be yes and your no be no. This helps to build integrity and character as well
- Take full responsibility for your actions. Stand up and be accountable; you are an adult
- Be very open about the matters that resulted in the mistrust in the initial onset
- In cases where professional or external help is needed to aid in the process, don't allow pride or selfishness to stand in the way. Your marriage is too vital to be sabotaged by these things. The pros far outweigh the cons

➤ Finally, ensure that you shower your spouse with love that is deep and pure

Lack of trust in a marriage is like a house that is built on sand and cannot stand, or a computer without the Central Processing Unit (CPU). It is parallel to a city whose walls are broken down and is left fully unprotected. Also, like a tottering fence that is not able to offer any protection or support to those on the inside. Let me take the time to list some of the devastating effects of lack of trust on a marriage.

Lack of trust affects marriage in the following ways:
➤ Causes a frail or weak marriage, because the foundation is missing a very vital building material
➤ Breeds insecurity between both spouses
➤ Affects meaningful communication
➤ Acts as a barrier to openness in expressing yourself to your spouse
➤ Results in fear, doubt, confusion, and selfishness
➤ Prevents oneness of the two spouses
➤ Negatively impacts mutual gratifying sex and intimacy, which is vital in this sacred union
➤ Greatly retards financial growth in a marriage
➤ Causes many break-ups, separations, and divorces
➤ Prevents a clear understanding of your spouse
➤ Keeps you in bondage
➤ Derails purpose and destiny in a marriage
➤ Aborts your vision for the growth of your marriage

As you can see, the lack of trust in a marriage is an enemy in many ways to this covenant relationship. Therefore, be vigilant in protecting your trust. Surprisingly, many married people are afraid to trust their spouses for various reasons.

Below are some of the reasons for this lack of trust:
➤ Fear of the unknown
➤ Afraid of being hurt, especially if they were already hurt in the past
➤ Fear of becoming known
➤ Fear of rejection
➤ Possess a judgemental attitude towards others
➤ Enough time is not spent on knowing his or her partner
➤ Reluctance, pride, and ignorance

- Lack of important disclosures and the withholding of vital information
- Inability to trust themselves first. If a person is not willing or able to trust himself, then he will not be able to extend trust to others. Trust breeds trust
- No open line of proper communication between spouses
- The existence of a mental block where one has basically erected a protective shield around his or her heart and emotions
- Trust is earned, so it is not innate. It takes much work. At times a spouse (or even both spouses) is not willing to put in the amount of work that is needed to develop trust in a marriage
- One of the spouses might have proven to be irresponsible and so cannot be entrusted with important matters
- One spouse may not trust the other due to that person's past negative behaviour, so there is the fear of recurrence
- Lack of reciprocity
- Lack of consistency in one's actions
- Over-reliance on oneself, as opposed to working together as a team
- Differences in religious and cultural beliefs
- Unforgiveness and the root of bitterness work negatively against trusting one's spouse

RECIPROCITY

Reciprocity, in general, requires that one's giving is contingent on what is received. Inequality is not held in high esteem in this case, in that you should give only what you have received. In the Bible, there are numerous examples of giving in relation to what one receives; for example, sowing and reaping, and tithing. However, reciprocity has both a negative and a positive component to it. In the case of marriage, reciprocity is employed here in a positive way. It has nothing to do with conditional giving and taking, but instead the showing or granting of mercy and grace to each other, whenever you have been wronged by the other. Neither does it mean that loving and sharing with each other should be conditional. It should not be hinged on whether you get back something in return for what you have done.

Mercy here involves showing compassion and offering forgiveness, even though you are able to do the opposite. Showing leniency or clemency to your spouse is of vital necessity. There are numerous times in your marriage when either of you will offend the other or be offended by the other. Both of you will always stand in need of mercy. In Matthew 5:7, we are told that "If we are merciful, then mercy will be bestowed upon us."

Grace, in the form of reciprocity, should therefore be extended to your spouse, even if at times he or she may not be deserving of it. Remember, grace is unmerited, and therefore should not be given on the basis of merit. Christ extends forgiveness to all of us daily, even when we are not deserving of it. Christ died for us, even though we are not worthy. Likewise, you should forgive, and you will be forgiven by God. If reciprocity is not active in the covenant relationship of marriage, then anger, strife, and bitterness will destroy its very foundation. A marriage that doesn't have a good and firm foundation will not last.

Lack of reciprocity is one of the factors that have contributed to the attacks against marriage. There is a serious lack of give-and-take as people try to get even with their spouse for wrongdoings. Unforgiveness has become the order of the day and has contributed considerably to the high divorce rate. People are prone to failure, but when your spouse fails, make a concerted effort to give-and-take as much as possible. Nevertheless, this should not be used as a license to commit evil.

In a marriage, you should be willing to reciprocate. You are not perfect; you are a work in progress. However, try to give and take with your spouse each day. You are going to need to forgive your spouse and also to be forgiven by your spouse.

IDENTIFY & EMBRACE THE DIFFERENCES IN EACH OTHER

Men, your spouse was made differently from you and vice versa. Our biological, physical, emotional, and psychological make-up is different. Men display and express their need for sex and intimacy differently from their wives. They tend to see sex as the only medium through which intimacy can be expressed. A man's ability to satisfy his wife sexually makes him feel a great sense of self-worth and improves his self-esteem. Men tend to establish their identity and their masculinity on their sexuality. They also tend to look at things from a different perspective on most occasions. God designed it that way. Most men will summarize an event in one word or by using a one-syllable word. Women, on the other hand, will give you a very detailed account of the same event, including date and time.

Take the time to identify and appreciate these differences in your spouse. This will enable you to better understand each other. Don't compete with each other; instead, you should complete each other. Combine your differences, weaknesses, and strengths for a successful marriage.

DON'T ALLOW THE SUN TO GO DOWN ON YOUR ANGER – SETTLE IT

Biblically and scientifically, it can be proven that men and women are made differently. Females are the weaker vessel. 1 Peter 3:7 says, *"Likewise, husbands, live with your wives in an understanding way, showing honour to the woman as the weaker vessel, since they are heirs with you of the grace of life, so that your prayers may not be hindered."* Due to these differences, disagreements will come, so pray continuously for grace to deal with them. Also, a family that spends the time to pray together is more likely to stay together. You should make it a part of your daily routine to pray with your spouse, as much as is humanly possible. This is highly important in a marriage. You will never regret it.

Learn to fight in prayer against the missiles pointed against your marriage. Prayer, and specifically prayer of agreement, can be a deadly weapon against the missiles sent out against this covenant relationship. When you approach the throne of God daily and cooperatively to seek God's direction and guidance for your life, it is quite rewarding. This helps to form an alliance against the kingdom of darkness. Also, when you pray for your spouse, this helps to strengthen the bond between the two of you. The sun should not go down with both of you angry with each other (Ephesians 4:26). Endeavour to do your daily spring cleaning in your marriage, even in the midst of winter. By so doing, you will facilitate and maintain a healthy marriage. Let go of those negative things behind you and move forward to positive and better things ahead of you. Don't hold each other hostage for the wrongs or disagreements of yesterday. Each day is a new day with new beginnings. Unforgiveness should not be allowed to become a stronghold in your marriage. This is destructive to both your life and your marriage, and will cause a breakdown in the family unit and ultimately cause divorce. Whichever position you hold in a disagreement, whether you are the offender or the victim, try to resolve the disagreement immediately. Don't allow the root of bitterness to spring up or take residence in your marriage. Don't allow unforgiveness to create blockages in your marriage, whether small or great. It is quite subtle and toxic, and its effects are far reaching. When offences come, because they will come, deal with them immediately and wisely. When you are forgiven by your spouse of an offence, learn how to receive that forgiveness. Stop feeling guilty for that wrong.

Unforgiveness blocks the release of God's favour upon your life. The way you treat your spouse has a lot to do with your prayers being answered. It will create disharmony in your marriage. It is important for you and your spouse to pray together, because if you do, then the likelihood of both of you staying together is very high. Now, two cannot pray unless they are in agreement, so if there is disharmony between the two of you then you will not get good results.

The root of bitterness should not be given a place in your marriage. It has destroyed many marriages and still continues to do so, daily. It manifests itself in the form of resentment, anger, and hatred for each other, thus destroying the unity that should be present. Bitterness is, in fact, a demonic spirit and, as with other spirits, it is always seeking for somewhere or someone to be contained in. Don't allow yourself or your marriage to be the vessel in which this tormenting spirit of bitterness resides. Instead, starve any trace of bitterness that tries to find itself in your life.

Forgiveness should be foundational in your marriage. If you cannot get past forgiving your spouse, this will prevent you from successfully getting to the next level, where your marriage will be joyful and rewarding. This is God's intention for your covenant relationship.

Bitterness causes a wall that divides you and your spouse. With the presence of bitterness, two hearts no longer beat as one. It is a form of defilement that prevents you from showing and receiving grace and mercy in your marriage. Bitterness is contagious. Therefore, if you allow it to be directed towards your spouse, then your spouse will eventually be infected by this poison. There are no benefits to be derived from accommodating bitterness in your marriage. If this is present, cut off its nutrients and allow it to die. Not only should you eliminate the bitterness in your marriage, but also ensure that you extract it from the root. By so doing, it will not spring again.

WAYS OF FIRING BACK AT THE ROOT OF BITTERNESS IN YOUR MARRIAGE

In order to excavate the root of bitterness, continuously forgive each other. Jesus commands us to forgive each other seventy times seven. He did this to show the level of grace that should be employed in our process of forgiveness. It should be indefinite, as it is almost impossible to keep track of the wrongs done against you. Forgiveness keeps no record of wrongs done. Also, vengeance belongs to God, and He promised to take care of it. Therefore, don't take on God's job; He has not asked you to. All He has asked you to do is to forgive. Replace bitterness with love for your spouse. Purpose in your heart to forgive your spouse as much as is humanly possible. You will stand in need of forgiveness from time to time.

Instead of bitterness, extend grace and mercy to your spouse, as you are being given these from day to day by God Himself. We can attest to the fact that we experience God's grace and mercy on a daily basis, even though we are not deserving of it. To eliminate any bitterness that you might have, first recognize that it is present and take corrective measures at the initial onset, before it becomes a stronghold. Whenever bitterness becomes a stronghold, there will be a reduction of love, joy, unity, and intimacy between you and your spouse. If bitterness is nurtured, then the very fabric of your marriage will be destroyed. Therefore, it is very important that you take the time to find out the root cause of the bitterness from your spouse's point of view. In addition, do a thorough self-examination. This is where divine intervention is extremely important and must be wisely sought after. Allow God's Word to become alive and active in your heart and life. His Word is like dynamite, and must be used to destroy or pluck out the root of bitterness.

After the root of bitterness is identified, don't allow fear, pride, or a combination of the two to prevent you from approaching your spouse and asking for forgiveness. It is highly recommended that you don't allow the sun to go down while you are still angry. In other words, settle your differences as quickly as possible and before retiring to bed, if possible.

There are some differences that you may not be able to settle before going to bed due to the nature of the problem. However, try to settle those as soon as possible. Don't allow too much time to elapse, because the bitterness will experience further growth, perhaps exponentially. Whenever this occurs, the level of love and intimacy that you are supposed to share will not be infringed upon. Don't give the devil entrance into your marriage by nurturing and accommodating the root of bitterness.

At this point in time, forgiveness will be imminent. Therefore, don't withhold forgiveness from your spouse, and don't be reluctant to receive the same from your spouse. Forgive so that your heavenly Father can in turn do likewise for you. Allow love to take its full course in this situation.

While addressing the root of bitterness caused by offences done by either party or both, desist from being offensive and defensive. Let humility be present while accepting and extending grace to each other. Grace is unmerited favour, therefore your spouse hasn't earned grace and neither have you. However, show or extend it to him or her anyways. Also, pray unceasingly for God's wisdom, direction, and enablement. Allow patience to do a perfect work in this situation. This is not an occasion or a platform for you to be pointing fingers at each other. Instead, it should be a time of identifying the problem and strategizing ways of dealing with it.

Starve bitterness by emphasizing the good in your spouse and how valuable he or she is to you. In other words, start seeing him or her the way God sees them. After you have forgiven your spouse of an offence against you, verbalize it. Let him or her know that he or she is forgiven of that offence. The same goes for the offender who is seeking forgiveness; be apologetic and remorseful. If you are the offended, don't become resentful of your spouse. This will eat away the very fabric of unity in your covenant relationship. Replace bitterness and unforgiveness in your marriage, and every other aspect of your life, with love and forgiveness. Remember, love blankets a multitude of sin, including those committed against you by your spouse. Don't allow evil to overcome you. Allow patience, compassion, kindness, and gentleness to have full course in your marriage. Endeavour to make your union be a portrait of these fruits, fully demonstrative of God's love.

The root of bitterness can only be totally rooted out by divine intervention and supernatural enablement. It should not be nurtured and allowed to grow. Whatever you nurture most will grow the fastest. Bitterness is demonic in nature and should not be given the opportunity to take up residence or become a stronghold in your life.

CHAPTER 5

DANGERS OF UNFORGIVENESS IN MARRIAGE

Unforgiveness in a marriage is synonymous to cancer in one's body. It's there to cause death to the body, and your marriage is no exception. If unforgiveness isn't dealt with speedily, it will cause a serious disconnect between you and your spouse, emotionally, sexually, spiritually, and otherwise.

There may be events in your past, including your childhood, that haven't been dealt with properly and successfully. As a result, the effects have spilled over into your marriage. Past experiences may include hurts from previous relationships that are still lingering in your heart and emotions. These problems can have a negative impact on your marriage, causing you to easily become angry and not give your spouse what he or she rightfully deserves. How you deal with these problems will determine the success you will achieve in your marriage. If you don't deal with these problems, they can result in constant conflict with your spouse.

If you are guilty of holding onto these past hurts and pains, it's imperative that you get spiritual and professional help. Not only must they be dealt with, but they must be dealt with successfully. Wisdom in dealing with past hurts is of paramount importance. Feelings of guilt will destroy your marriage, if they haven't already done so. Use your bitterness to get better. Although your experiences might have been bitter, use them as stepping stones to get better. In other words, don't be stuck in that bitter past.

If left untreated, unforgiveness will affect our entire being and cause a breakdown in your emotions. It is like a little leaven that affects a whole loaf of bread. Unforgiveness is highly detrimental to marriage. Malignant issues from the past can silently eat away at you, until your marriage dies, emotionally, and even physically. Unforgiveness can become deeply rooted in a person, almost to the point of being invisible, until the signs suddenly become visible. It can cause serious health problems, including depression and cancer. Not forgiving someone will negatively impact your relationships, both present and future, and ultimately affect your destiny. In other words, unforgiveness hinders the creation and maintenance of a healthy relationship, including marriage.

Pay great attention to the initial onset of unforgiveness; don't give it the opportunity to become deeply rooted in your soul. Allowing this will result in the development of the root of bitterness, causing defilement. Un forgiveness can also negatively affect those around you. It will hold you in bondage as a prisoner. It has the potential to prevent you from living life to the fullest, and hold you back from maximizing your true potential. Unforgiveness is, in fact, an open door for Satan to enter your marriage and be a part of your relationship. He is then at liberty to take advantage of your covenant relationship. Our prayers will also be hindered, because God honours His Word above His name; His Word is His bond.

Whenever you are prevented from bearing the spiritual fruit of love, it can cause you to hate your spouse. You will experience fear due to the absence of perfect love. In addition, unforgiveness will cause a lack of trust in your spouse, even though he or she is quite deserving of it. Trust is a vital, foundational element of marriage. I strongly believe that two cannot walk together unless they trust each other, especially in a covenant relationship. A lack of trust will prevent you from becoming cemented in your marriage as you ought to. You won't be bonded emotionally, sexually, physically, spiritually, or otherwise with your spouse. When you are not bonded sexually in your marriage, you will not be able to enjoy the pleasures that God has given freely to married couples. Sex and intimacy will not be rewarding for you.

Unforgiveness in marriage will also result in constant fighting, either verbally or physically. It has contributed to terrible breakdowns in the family unit, and has often led to divorce. Unforgiveness is a spiritual problem and can only be dealt with effectively by prayer and fasting; not the simple kind of prayer but the "sackcloth and ashes" type of prayer. The spirit of unforgiveness has a possessive tendency and easily becomes a stronghold. It is indeed a heavy weight to carry around and will also result in exhaustion and sickness. Unforgiveness will negatively impact the quality of sex and intimacy in a marriage. If you hold bitterness against your spouse, you will not be able to enjoy the joy and pleasure that should occur in a marriage. You will not be able to love your spouse as you ought to. Love keeps no record of wrongs (1 Corinthians 13:5). If unforgiveness is left untreated, it will totally eradicate the vital component of love in your relationship.

Whenever unforgiveness is given a chance to become a stronghold, you are setting a precedence for your children to follow. Children live what they learn, and your life is one of their greatest teachers. If you paint a portrait of unforgiveness, then they will emulate it. They tend to see their parents as their heroes. Therefore, if you model a lack of forgiveness, you will soon become a champion of unforgiveness.

The spirit of unforgiveness causes the hardening of the heart and allows torment to take place. This infringes greatly upon the peace that we should share and enjoy. Unforgiveness has resulted in numerous crimes being committed between spouses, including murder. This is due to the hatred that accompanies unforgiveness. This gives the devil an entrance and a stronghold in our lives and marriages. Forgiveness, on the other hand, will prevent Satan from entering our hearts, lives, and marriages. When Jesus taught His disciples to pray, He included the concept of asking the father to forgive their sins as they forgive those who have wronged them. If you are not willing to allow forgiveness to take its full course in your marriage, then this will prevent you and your spouse from operating in oneness and connecting spiritually, sexually, and emotionally. Fight assiduously, with God at the forefront of this battle, to rid your marriage of unforgiveness.

Reasons for Unforgiveness

Ignorance is one of the major reasons why forgiveness is not extended to the offender, because the offended doesn't know how to move from the point of being wronged to the placed of being liberated from those wrongs. It is difficult because they are trying to do so in their own strength, which is humanly impossible. As mentioned before, forgiveness is a supernatural act of God.

Our willingness to forgive can only be dealt with by the Holy Spirit. There are times when one is so badly hurt and scarred by offences that it takes the Holy Spirit to do a work of forgiveness. The act of forgiveness is divine in nature. It is natural for mankind to be reluctant to forgive each other. Therefore, we are not capable of forgiving until God adds His supernatural to our natural. At times, we fail to forgive because of our inability to acknowledge God's forgiveness towards us also.

Other times, we remain stuck in the past as opposed to getting past our past and entering the present. Forget your past and give way to the birthing of a new day in your life. Grace and mercy have been extended to you by God on a continuous basis, and to others, including your spouse. Guard your heart and mind against unforgiveness by not focusing on the wrongs committed against you. The inability to truly place value on our relationships with others will stand as an obstacle to forgiveness. The root cause of this is the absence of the love of God in our heart.

Some people also refuse to forgive others who have wronged them because they don't fully understand the negative impact it has upon them. This causes damage to their social, physical, emotional, and spiritual health. Unforgiveness will destroy your relationship with God and also with your spouse. You will not be able to love and please God, or your spouse, in a meaningful way. If you are refusing to forgive your fellowman, then your heavenly Father cannot lie, He has no choice but to withhold forgiveness from you also.

Pride is also a factor that fuels unforgiveness. If you refuse to forgive, you are actually believing that the offender is not worthy of your forgiveness. This can be due to the nature and severity of the offence committed against you. Sometimes, the offence was not even directly committed against you, but against someone that you love and care about. Remember, the truth is, you are also not worthy of God's love and forgiveness, yet He forgives you anyway. He extends this to you in the form of grace and mercy. Think about that.

Some people are reluctant to forgive because they don't want to be seen in a position of powerlessness. In other words, they don't want to be portrayed by others as being weak. Some men believe if they forgive, they may become vulnerable to being dominated by their wife. Also, they may not want their friends, relatives, and associates to see them in that manner. Hence, they may be afraid to forgive, especially if they were significantly hurt before.

CHAPTER 6

BENEFITS OF FORGIVENESS IN MARRIAGE

Forgiveness enables you to let go of any form of bitterness that may be lodging in your heart. It means to dismiss wrongs done against you and offer pardon to the wrongdoer. You cannot truly forgive by your own strength. Forgiveness gives God a chance to work in you and through you to reach out to your spouse in a joyful way. Also, it relieves you of any form of pain and the scars of the past. Forgiveness enables you to restore your spouse to their former position as if no offence was committed against you. Indeed, it restores unity and intimacy in this blessed union. Forgiveness is quite soothing and highly therapeutic, in that whatever pain was inflicted upon you will no longer continue to hold you in bondage. You will experience the joy that comes from God, which does not change. Forgiveness also allows your spirit to become free, so you can experience the peace of God in all areas of your life. What a place of rest to be in.

Whenever forgiveness is active in your marriage, the level of love and intimacy in your marriage will not be infringed upon. Both you and your spouse will be able to relate to each other in a pleasurable and rewarding way, sexually. Men, cleaving to your wives as you have become one flesh will also be easier, because you will be better able to love your wives as God intended.

Salvation is founded on love and forgiveness. It was love that drove Jesus to the cross with the objective to forgive and redeem mankind back to himself after the fall of Adam in the Garden of Eden. That is the extent to which He loves us; He gave His life for us. Although He did, we continue to sin against Him on a daily basis, and He continues to forgive us. Therefore, we should in turn forgive others, including our spouses. We, ourselves, stand in need of forgiveness, daily. Forgiveness is good for both our spiritual and natural wellbeing.

Forgiveness enables you to release those who have hurt you and also to release God's hand to fulfill His promises that He has made to you. By so doing, you unblock your prayers that unforgiveness has blocked. Be willing to forget the past and move on. The Word of God tells us that vengeance is His, and He will repay (Romans 12:19). God will give justice, and remember, justice is not necessarily good but what one rightfully deserves. He has asked us to become fishers of men, and that will only happen if we forgive those who have wronged us. This can potentially lead to reconciliation of broken down relationships, including marriage.

Forgiveness will take you out of a place where you are controlled by others. Unforgiveness causes anger. Whenever someone is able to anger you, then they actually control you and hold you in bondage. God Himself has forgiven us and still continues to do so, daily. We must forgive others so that God will not hold us guilty, and so that our prayers are not hindered. You can release the offender and in turn release yourself so that God's hands can be visible in your situation.

Whenever forgiveness occurs, you open the door for restoration to take place. When this happens, the offender is brought back to the original state before he or she had committed the offence against you. When Adam sinned, God sent His Son to reconcile us back to Himself. Here, the door was swung open for you to be restored. You only have to choose to walk through that door. You should forgive to cancel the wrong that the offender has done to you. It is like the cancellation of a financial debt against a debtor. You write it off your books, and it is no longer held against the name of that person. Therefore, you set the debtor free. In this case, we set ourselves free as well. Forgiveness places you in a position where you can accept forgiveness from your spouse and others. It is enables restoration and reconciliation.

It is extremely important that we guard our minds. Don't allow negative thoughts and unforgiveness into your thought patterns. Instead, occupy your thoughts with forgiveness and positive thoughts, because there are more benefits to be derived from doing so.

CHAPTER 7

FIGHTING BACK
STOP PLAYING THE BLAMING GAME

Take responsibility for your actions and stop blaming your spouse, or others, when you do wrong. Husband (Adam) stop blaming your wife (Eve) for going against God's command. Also, stop blaming God for the wife He gave you. In other words, if you are wrong, confess it and repent of it. After you have done so, don't return to your former sinful action.

Wives, stop blaming your husband for your prohibited actions. Also, stop trying to change your spouse; instead, work on your own actions that may be creating problems in your marriage. It is not your duty to change your husband.

Show respect to your spouse, including their different viewpoints in a conversation. You will not always agree; however, you should respectfully disagree.

PRAY UNCEASINGLY

Pray unceasingly for God to give you a spiritual awakening to the value He places on marriage. Marriage deserves honour; stop desecrating it. Pray daily for your spouse, marriage, and family so that you will know how to love your spouse unconditionally. Employ the supernatural power of God to forgive your spouse and not hold a grudge against him or her. Allow your marriage to exemplify truth, dedication, commitment, and faithfulness.

This vicious attack that is launched against marriage can only be won with intense prayer and fasting. The missiles are continuous and they are coming from several different angles and in different forms. Supernatural intervention is needed to win this battle. Remember, you are in a battle, and your only sword is the Word of God. Don't hesitate to draw upon it and use it effectively in your marriage. Guard your marital gate with intense prayer. You cannot afford to have your gate unguarded, or else you will be plundered by the enemy of this holy ordinance.

MAINTAIN SEXUAL INTIMACY

Sex in marriage should not be viewed in a negative light, especially by people of faith. You should not withhold sexual intimacy from your spouse, except in the case where both of you have come to an agreement for a specified period of time in order to fast and pray, or due to medical reasons (1 Corinthians 7:5). Otherwise, it is ungodly if not done within this context. God designed sex and intimacy to be an integral part of marriage. He honours sexual intimacy within the parameters of marriage. You have a God-given responsibility to satisfy your spouse sexually. Sex is meant to be gratifying for both you and your spouse. Sex and intimacy also fosters further sexual growth, which is a very vital part of marriage.

Couples need to be properly educated on the true value of sex and intimacy in this covenant relationship. With proper education, one will dismiss the myth held by many people of faith that sex is dirty. Sex is only wrong outside of marriage. Anything that God places honour on, don't try to dishonour it.

After you have gotten married, you are no longer your own, and you no longer have the right over your own body—your spouse does. Your sexual involvement must be with your spouse only. Keep your body holy unto God, and stay away from adultery and other sexual impurities. In addition, don't allow selfishness to enter your marriage. Instead, each of you should be mindful of each other's needs, including sexual needs, and strive to fulfill them.

What a pleasurable moment it is when a man and his wife come together and share sexual intimacy. It is quite a rewarding and fulfilling experience that tightens the bond between them. Sex and intimacy can be compared to the cement that helps to hold this bond together. Therefore, I implore you to endeavour to restore and maintain the passion of sex and intimacy in your marriage.

From a Christian perspective, intimacy in marriage encompasses one's total being—physically, emotionally and spiritually. This cannot be fully explained by humans, because it is not our doing. Biblically, sex and intimacy are built on the holiness and faithfulness of a married couple. It is designed by God to be shared between both parties in a marriage covenant. When God gave this gift to mankind, one of His intents was to bring happiness to the union.

Sex is the only medium through which a married couple can fulfill God's command to be fruitful and multiply. Sex and intimacy in a marriage can prevent either party from indulging in sexual sin. However, many indulge in extramarital affairs. As part of our biological composition, we are all naturally inclined to be intimate with the opposite sex, so God made that provision. The passion for intimacy is met when both persons in a marriage fulfill their moral obligations to each other. If either party suffers from a medical condition that prevents them from being sexually satisfying to each other, take the time out to seek the necessary medical attention.

There are cases where the enthusiasm to be sexually satisfying to one's spouse is lacking due to certain factors. Life's challenges, hard, long hours of work, and family commitments are some of the major reasons. These sometimes cause one to be extremely tired and exhausted, resulting in reduced enthusiasm. Couples should endeavour to put things in the proper perspective, and prioritize. The sexual flame in a marriage should not be compromised for frivolous reasons. In other words, be passionate about your sex life in your marriage.

A marriage cannot be consummated, unless there is a sexual encounter between a man and his wife. When a marriage is consummated, it becomes perfect or complete in the eyes of God. This helps to cement both husband and wife together.

Acquiring mutual sexual fulfilment in marriage might not flow naturally for some people. Therefore, it may require a bit of work initially. Some people need more work than others. It is very important that couples, especially newly married couples, understand that patience is indeed a virtue.
In Deuteronomy 24:5, after a couple enters a marital covenant, they were required to isolate themselves from society and be together alone for a period of one year. The purpose of this was for them to learn more about each other and be bonded together as one flesh. This is indicative of the fact that a couple needs to spend quality time together. Mutual sexual fulfilment is a learnt behaviour that comes with much practice. People also learn at different paces, so some may take longer to master the art of gratifying their spouse sexually. Be patient with each other. Do not allow frustration, discouragement, or confusion to set into this integral area of your marriage. If you allow that to happen, it could cause, and has caused, a breakup or even a divorce.

Let's journey over to Genesis 2:24, where God performed the first marriage. He intended for both a man and his wife to be joined together, thus becoming one flesh. Although sexual intimacy appears to only be a physical act, it has a deep spiritual truth to it. It is the conduit that facilitates a deep love between a man and his wife. Sexual intimacy is a medium through which a couple gives themselves to each other selflessly to obtain mutual sexual fulfilment. Therefore, it must be entered into with the right attitude and without self-centeredness.

I want to further expound the purposes and the importance of sexual intimacy in marriage, the way God designed it. Sex is the medium through which procreation becomes possible. From the beginning of time, God instructed Adam and Eve to multiply. The replenishing of the earth with humans is only possible through this process. This is a divine process. God's original plan for marriage was that two virgins should come together in marriage. According to the custom in the Old Testament, after that takes place, and on the night of the wedding, the marriage should be consummated, and the couple would sleep on a white sheet. During that consummation process, the hymen should break and blood should come forth due to the broken hymen. This would prove that the female is a virgin. The hymen is defined by the Oxford Dictionary as "a fold of mucous membrane that partly covers the entrance to the vagina, and is usually ruptured when sexual intercourse takes place for the first time." When the hymen breaks, blood from the vagina flows over the male sexual organ, which then consummates, or makes complete, the blood covenant made between both the man and the woman. On the morning after the wedding, the sheet was presented to the elders, and if the white sheet on which both of them laid was not spotted or stained with blood, then the woman would be stoned.

Under the Mosaic Law, a divorce would only be granted if the man could successfully separate his blood from his wife's blood that flowed during the consummation of their marriage. This is highly impossible to do. Therefore, this indicates that God intends for the covenant relationship of marriage to be for life. The sexual relationship between a man and his wife is synonymous to the relationship between Jesus Christ and His Church. In like manner, as Christ possesses pure, deep love for His Church, so should a man love his wife. The Church must be in submission to Jesus Christ, and the same holds true for the wife to her own husband. Men, when you love your wife, you will be able to give of yourselves selflessly to her. Women, when you are in submission to your husband, giving of yourselves will not pose a problem. This oneness that is supposed to be achieved after a man leaves his parents and cleaves to his wife is intended to mirror the relationship between Christ and His Church. It is also an indication of the oneness, from a spiritual perspective, that this type of relationship should have.

APPRECIATE AND RESTORE THE SANCTITY OF MARRIAGE

Whenever the sanctity of marriage is desecrated, it creates a chain reaction that affects generations to come. God spoke expressly that marriage is honourable. If you dishonour this institution by committing whoredom or adultery, He will judge you for such a sin, especially if not repented of. Whoredom happens when one is single and carries out sexual activities, while adultery occurs when one is married and has sexual relations with someone other than one's spouse.

Marriage is a holy and divine covenant, not a contract. It is binding, and creates a bond between the two parties who have entered into it. Its divinity must not be replaced by a prenuptial agreement. Much work needs to be done to ensure that the foundational features of marriage—love, trust, and reciprocity—return to marriage. It is extremely important that the family unit be restored and preserved. God is very much interested in the family unit, because this is where the nurturing and caring of one's offspring should take place. It is the platform whereby children should be raised up in the fear and admonition of the Lord. Marriage is where children should be taught to love and obey their parents and others. Also, they should be taught to show respect to others, especially those in authority.

The purposes for which marriage was instituted by God must be highly esteemed. When God designed marriage, He did it quite purposefully. It was not good for man to be alone from the beginning of time, and then woman was created for companionship and for procreation. After a man leaves his parents and is joined in marriage, he should ensure that he also cleaves to his wife, and her only. This will enable them to become one flesh, as God has intended for them.

In addition, marriage is clean, so keep it clean. Don't accommodate any foreign body in your union, or it will become infected, and potentially die. The human body is naturally designed to fight off bad bacteria. However, there are certain types of bacteria which, if found in the body, will result in the breakdown of the immune system. If treatment is not immediate and radical, this kind of bacteria will eventually become fatal. Likewise, when a foreign body attacks a marriage, this attack should not be taken lightly. Immediate and radical actions are needed to rid this invasion before it becomes fatal. Foreign bodies enter your marriage to derail your marital train, change your course, break down the family unit, and eventually kill your marriage by tearing your union asunder.

FLEE SEXUAL IMMORALITY

Fulfill your sexual duties to your spouse. The Bible implores us to not allow promiscuity, adultery, and other forms of sexual immorality to be named among us. Remember, God is jealous when His people go after other gods. Marriage is like that relationship of love and commitment between God and His Church. Therefore, when you step outside of your marriage covenant and participate in such immoral acts, you are desecrating this holy ordinance. Adultery defiles marriage and violates this holy ordinance. Matthew 19:9 states that adultery is committed when someone is divorced and marries another. When someone divorces his wife for a reason other than sexual unfaithfulness and marries another, then adultery is committed by that person. Then, the person who marries the one who was put away also commits adultery.

In 1 Corinthians 6:18-20, we are instructed not to allow sexual immorality to reign in our bodies. Your body is a place for God to dwell, and He cannot dwell or tabernacle in an unclean vessel. Your body is not yours, but was lent to you by God. Therefore, you are accountable to Him for whatever activities you have done in your body. You must live in a manner that will give glory to God. Your marriage should mirror the bond that exists between the Church and Jesus Christ.

The Book of Hebrews speaks about the honour that is due to marriage. If you engage in sexual activities outside of your marriage, you will defile the marital bed. Stop defiling this bed, because it is meant to be undefiled. Adultery demands a very high price, without any dividend. This price could be the loss of your relationship with your God and your spouse, total devastation and the breakdown of your family unit, or divorce.

In addition, both adultery and fornication are the main causes in the spread of sexually transmitted diseases. Many have died due to these diseases. Adultery and fornication also put you into spiritual bondages and generate unholy connections between a man's soul and that of a harlot. Demons are transferrable, so be careful who and what you get connected with.

Pornography should not replace your commitment to be faithful in your marriage. Pornography involves being physically unfaithful to your spouse. You should endeavour to guard what you watch, because the eye is the medium through which we are enticed, then tempted, and finally drawn away into lust. Your eye is the first point of entry into your mind. Even if you have not physically participated in the act of adultery or fornication, the fact that you have lusted after it means you have sinned, and you are, therefore, guilty. Flea fornication and allow your body to be a vessel of honour. Let holiness abound in you and have its free flow.

In addition, pornography will give you wild and unrealistic desires that cannot be fulfilled by your spouse. Whenever this happens, conflict will arise and you will start looking outside of that covenant relationship for sexual gratification. Your body is the temple of God; don't desecrate it. Sex done within the context of marriage is holy, and unless the standard of holiness is upheld, you cannot see God.

Other forms of sexual immorality are rape, incest, homosexuality, pederasty, bestiality, and pedophilia. All these are abominations to the Lord.

RAPE
The Bible says that a man should have his own wife. By so doing, he should render due benevolence to his wife, and vice versa. In other words, only be sexually involved with the person that you are in covenant with.

INCEST
We are instructed in the Bible not to participate in incest. You should never *"uncover the nakedness"* of a relative or someone who is related to you (Leviticus 18:6). It is an abomination in the sight of God. Desist from committing such immoral acts.

HOMOSEXUALITY & PEDERASTY
Homosexuality is the case where a man lies with another as he would with a woman. This also goes for a woman lying with another woman as she would with a man (Leviticus 18:22). In the Garden of Eden, when God saw that man was lonely, He provided the solution to man's loneliness by removing one of Adam's ribs to make Eve. Man, your rib was placed into a woman. Homosexuality has been a major contributing factor in the destruction of the family unit. Marriages have ended up in divorce due to the same (Leviticus 18:22-30; 20:3).
Pederasty involves an adult male having sexual involvement with a young boy. This is another fire that marriage is under.

BESTIALITY
Bestiality is another form of sexual immorality. The Word of God clearly stipulates that you should not "lie or stand before a beast," for it is an abomination (Leviticus 18:23).
All these immoral acts are not what God intended for mankind. When you deviate from God's way, He warns that He is a jealous God. Start embracing the Word of God, and let it be evident in your marriage. This covenant is built on the principles of God, with a great deal of love, commitment, faithfulness, and truth. God's authority is final and takes pre-eminence over the norms of our day. It must be respected, even in the sexuality and intimacy in your marriage.

PEDOPHILIA
This is a case where an adult or an adolescent is sexually attracted to children. If you bear the guilt of this, repent immediately and cease and desist from doing it.

KEEP OPEN LINES OF COMMUNICATION WITH YOUR SPOUSE

It is of vital importance that an open line of communication is maintained between you and your spouse. Openly discuss issues that bother you; if you don't, you will become toxic. Silence doesn't necessarily mean consent. Listen twice as much as you talk, that's possibly the reason why we have two ears and only one mouth. Also, the tongue is a deadly instrument, and it contains power to the extent of life and death in it. Keep it under subjection, as it can destroy generations.

Honesty and transparency are also two other very important features in keeping open lines of communication, especially in a marriage. Ensure that both you and your spouse are clear on a matter. You should strive to be in agreement. However, there are times when you will disagree, but don't allow this gap to get too wide. At the same time, respect each other's view on a matter that is important.

Keep an open line of communication between God and your marriage. It is not an option that you seek guidance and direction from God for your union, because there are many unique issues that you will experience. These issues can only be dealt with through supernatural intervention, so allow God to add His supernatural to your natural.

Don't become guilty of the case of being present yet absent. Put your all into your marriage for it to work. Marriage is not a one-sided case; it is a covenant that needs both parties to be a part of it. Remember, part of the wedding vow states "Until death do we part." Men, when God sanctions you to leave your parents, who are most dear to you, it shows that others who are not your spouse should be placed in the "left behind" category. Having an open line of communication with those people will corrupt your marriage.

When you don't take the time to communicate in your marriage, it can lead to great resentment when you are dissatisfied about something. If the dissatisfaction is not verbalized and remains buried, it can cause two who were once fitly joined together to become disjointed and to eventually fall apart. If something is bothering you in your marriage, sit down together and talk about it. Talk is free. Your spouse is most likely not a psychic, nor is he or she a prophet or prophetess who can decipher what is bothering you. Therefore, take time to communicate with your spouse every day. This is one way you will get to know each other more. Learn the art of proper communication. Remember that throughout this process there is an encoder and a decoder. More importantly, communication is incomplete if the message communicated is not understood by both.

It is very important that you communicate with transparency. Endeavour to understand your spouse. Miscommunication has destroyed many marriages, and still continues to do so. Don't take communicating with each other for granted. Communication can be both verbal and nonverbal. During the process of communication, endeavour to be a good listener. Listen twice as much as you talk. Too little communication, as well as too much communication, has destroyed marriages. The bottom line is to know when to take a temporary break from talking about a subject matter that concerns you or your spouse.

In addition, pay attention to how you communicate. At times, it's not what is said but how it is said. Before you communicate with your spouse, assess the time and the environment in which to do so. Ask yourself these questions: Is this the right timing and the right environment for this conversation? Are they conducive to what I'm going to communicate to my spouse?

While communicating verbally, remember that the tongue, though so small, is quite deadly in nature. Pay great attention to your body language during the process; it has a tendency to speak louder than what you are saying. It is necessary that you learn how to communicate with your spouse. Disagreements will come, but you must learn how to disagree with each other respectfully, without any form of aggression. Take the time out to learn and master the art of conflict resolution. As mentioned before, pray unceasingly.

CHAPTER 8

WARNINGS FOR THE MARRIED AND UNMARRIED

TO THE MARRIED

Remember, marriage is honourable and should not accommodate any outsiders; keep it holy. Marriage is not triangular in nature. It is like a circle that is made up of two halves, one for each of you. Its edges are circular, so it cannot accommodate any foreign bodies hanging onto it. These foreign bodies are highly bacterial in nature and only have destructive capabilities, so keep it clean.

Hitchhikers may come in the form of your next door neighbours, co-workers, best friends, family friends, bosses, and so forth. Whatever format they have taken on, they are destructive to this holy union of marriage. For those who are married, especially Christians, don't kid yourselves, you cannot expect to take up fire in your bosom and not be burned. Infidelity will take you further than you planned to go. Most hitchhikers don't have a set destination. They are only there to hitch a ride for the moment to where your train can take them. Also, there are some with a destination and hitchhike on your train to get where they are going. Remember, these ones are not in it for the long haul; they either jump off or fall off the train at some point in time. They were not meant to be there in the first place. They were not a part of God's initial plan for your sacred union. The objective of hitchhikers is universal and transcends time and geographical locations. In other words, hitchhikers are never willing to pay the cost of getting to their destination; they are just looking for a free ride. In fact, they have not invested anything valuable in or for this journey, so they have nothing to lose after derailing your train. After jumping off your train, their next quest is to look for another train that has a destination with passengers who have paid their way on this journey. Totally pathetic, isn't it?

Presumably, you have voluntarily enlisted yourself in this army of marriage that has rules, policies, and guidelines slated by God Himself and must be followed carefully. Some of these guidelines are as follows: "Husbands love your wives as Christ loved the Church and gave Himself for it," (Ephesians 5:25) and "A man shall leave his parents and be joined to his wife and become one flesh" (Genesis 2:24). Therefore, you can only become one flesh with your wife, not a concubine.

Men, the Bible warns of being involved in fornication, as you can ignorantly develop unholy soul ties with a harlot. A soul tie is spiritual and can keep you bound, because you are joined with this harlot, not in a covenant relationship, but as one flesh. Whenever this occurs, you have committed sin against your own body. The same is applicable to adultery. The development of these unholy soul ties can be quite catastrophic, because the demonic spirit that is present in that person is transferrable to you.

To my female counterparts, some of the guidelines for marriage are as follows: "Wives, submit yourself to your own husbands," (Ephesians 5:22) not to anyone else. Just for the sake of clarity, this does not mean to become a door mat; you are one of God's prized possessions. As a wife, you are not in the least exempt from loving your husband to the extent that God commissioned us to do. It is of vital importance that you do so. A marriage cannot survive or withstand the test of time without love. In marriage, true love enables you to weather the storms of life and the contrary winds that will blow.

Marriage also comes with a uniform and some instructions to keep your body holy, for it is God's temple, and you are accountable for whatever unrighteousness is done within it. Now that you have enlisted yourself, hopefully voluntarily, in this army, please wear the uniform well with dignity, irrespective of where you are and with whom. Don't forget who you are and whose you are. Don't bring disgrace on the family of God and His army, or to your earthly family that God has given to you. If you are a male, then you are commissioned to be the head, so ask God for wisdom to lead your family to victory.

Marriage is like a train. As you travel daily, pay close attention to free-loaders and hitchhikers. Also, pay close attention to biblical principles; they are there to direct your train safely to success. It is absolutely necessary that you observe the warning signs that hitchhikers are trying to derail your train. Some of these signs are frequent phone calls, either to your home or your spouse's cell phone; the extreme closeness of your spouse to another party, especially of the opposite sex; or the frequent mentioning of the hitchhiker's name in your family conversations. These are, in fact, warning signs; don't ignore them, as they point to a precipice along the road. In addition, when your spouse is no longer available to dine at home, it could be a sign that they are doing take-outs. On this premise, I will caution the prey of the hitchhiker to be careful where you dine, as your destination can cause you to lose your vision, strength (like Sampson in the Bible) and, ultimately, your destiny in God.

Hitchhikers don't even care if they get killed in the process of derailment. All they are concerned about is getting the free ride without paying the cost of getting to their destination. The demons of adultery and fornication have blinded their eyes, so they are unable to see that they should not put asunder what God has put together. God is so serious about His Word that He would allow Heaven and Earth to pass away before one of His words go unfulfilled.

Do not touch or taste the unclean things of adultery. You are in a covenant with God and your spouse. Simply put, you are not your own. At times, you may be cornered by "Potiphar's wife," but be like Joseph and run, even if your garment is left behind, don't tarry. I warn you, don't delay; this could be dangerous. Remember, when evil appears, run or walk away from it. By so doing, you will be securing the eternal destiny for your soul.

In addition, be careful where along the road of your marriage you stop and ask directions, or where you detour from the main road. Remember that one of the duties of the hitchhiker is to derail your train, which can result in serious casualties. If you stop to get directions along the way, pay close attention to who gives you instructions. The bottom line is don't walk in the council of the ungodly or the unproductive. Even though you may get tired along the journey, be careful not to go to sleep in the arms of Delilah, you will wake up without your locks, strength, and sight. If you don't believe it, ask Sampson. You will lose it all.

I want to reiterate the following:
- Marriage is honourable; don't dishonour it.
- Marriage is holy; keep it clean.
- Beware of hitchhikers hanging on to your marriage. They are only there for a free ride.
- You should both submit yourselves to each other by mutually loving each other, unconditionally and sacrificially.

TO THE UNMARRIED

Marriage is a covenant between a male and a female. It should not be entered into lightly, neither should it be taken for granted or as an opportunity to be capitalized on. It is a covenant that is not meant to be broken, except on the grounds of unfaithfulness. Although it is sacred and more serious than enlisting into a country's army, it is analogous to joining the army, in some areas. Once you have decided to enlist in this army called marriage, it is advisable that you seek divine intervention and guidance about whom you will be joined together with in holy matrimony. Don't lose sight of the fact that love should be the nucleus in this joining process.

This sacred covenant involves hard work and dedication. One has to be prepared to give of oneself selflessly to the other party, until death. Now, this is a serious covenant, not a contract. This covenant is divine, as opposed to a contract that is drafted up by man. God performed the first marriage Himself in the Garden of Eden. This highlights the fact that He is a part of this covenant relationship and should not be left out. If you leave Him out, it is like going to battle without a commander-in-chief.

If you are hoping to get married, be prepared to love unconditionally, give of yourself selflessly to your spouse, and recognize God as the head of your marriage. Also, be prepared to fight relentlessly against the spirit that is fighting against marriage. The missiles being launched are many, and they are forceful. You must be willing not to become a casualty in this battle. Put on the whole armour of God (Ephesians 6:10-17). And after you have done all, stand on guard.

CHAPTER 9

WORDS OF WISDOM TO MEN AND WOMEN

TO MEN

Men, you ought to be respectful to your wives. Treat your wife with dignity, and be loyal to her. It is also very important that you are conscious of what her needs are, and are willing to cater to those needs. There is still a little girl in her that needs to be loved, hugged, and treated gently. Don't forget to embrace that little girl in her.

Be vigilant and guard your marriage, because the Delilah spirit is still out to get her prey, Sampson, so be careful whose lap you are sleeping in and what secrets you are disclosing. If you are not careful, you will wake up without your strength, vision, and a severed relationship with your God and family. Brothers, be vigilant because the woman of Samaria is now dead, but her spirit is still roaming the earth. When Jesus asked her for her husband, she rightly said she had none, because she had several, and even the one she was living with was not her own.

Adultery is a spirit that has infested marriages from the beginning of time, but now has reached crisis proportions, regrettably even in Christendom. It is like a pandemic, so to ensure that you don't get contaminated by it, put on the whole armour of God. The purpose of armour is to protect you from dangers during a battle. You are in a war against the sprits that are firing against marriage. You are encouraged to put on this armour entirely. The devil knows that when marriages are destroyed, generations to come will be affected.

As a soldier you cannot wear the uniform without wearing the necessary gear. Putting on the armour of God involves the following (Ephesians 6:11-18):

Helmet of Salvation

This helmet will help you to focus your mind on God's will regarding honouring your marriage covenant. It will prevent Satan from having a stronghold on your thoughts. You will not be enticed by pornography and other immoral acts, and neither will you envy your neighbour's wife. In other words, guard your mind against immoral and illicit acts. Your head is similar to a CPU in a computer. If the CPU is corrupt and dysfunctional, then the computer cannot function properly. In this case, if you allow your head to become contaminated, then the result will be devastating.

Loins Gird About with Truth

Use the Word of God skillfully. Allow truth to have its full course in your heart, life, and marriage. After you have entered into this covenant, be truthful to your spouse and to others, especially strange women. Whenever you come in contact with a strange woman, don't conceal the fact that you are married. Please wear this uniform proudly and truthfully. Remember, you are no longer your own; you are one of two halves. Also, you are in a covenant, so honour it wherever you go, even if this fact is not known to others.

Sword of the Spirit

This is, in fact, the Word of God. As a soldier in combat for your marriage, keep your sword in hand and be ready to fight. You cannot afford to put your sword down until the enemy that's warring against marriage is destroyed. You should be both offensive and defensive in this case. Marriage is honourable before God, so fight assiduously.

Men, be vigilant and defensive for your marriage. Remember, you are expected to serve from a position of headship in your marriage. Therefore, guard its gates with fasting and prayer. Take continuous inventory of how well the gates are guarded to ensure that you are following covenant principles. Also, learn the ways of Jezebel and Delilah, so that you will not be named amongst the statistics of men who have slept in their laps and have lost their hair, eyes, and strength. Don't sell out the secrets of your covenant and your family to strange women. They are not God's design for your marriage.

In addition, learn the characteristics of those persons who are destructive to your marriage, so that you can strategically walk among them without getting into illicit relationships with them. You are in covenant with your spouse, who is the only person in this covenant. Don't walk as fools, but as wise men, and don't forget to redeem the time in which you are living.

Breastplate of Righteousness

Righteousness will exalt a nation, including your household. Wherever this key component is missing, reproach will take its place. Let the breastplate of righteousness be worn at all times. It is a protective gear for your heart that allows holiness to take its full course. Your heart was given to your spouse in the marriage covenant, not to strange women. Guard it with diligence, because it is out of the heart that the issues of life flow (Proverbs 4:23). Also, keep it pure by paying close attention to what you allow to enter.

You were given only one heart, so it cannot adequately be shared with more than one person. You should have given it to your spouse when you entered into marriage.

TO WOMEN

Women, be reminded that you should be in submission to your own husband. In other words, show respect for his leadership, especially in the family. I will say that submission does not mean that you are any less of a person. Submission does not imply that you should not be an active participant in the decision-making process in the family or the running of the household. Your wise input should be given and should be respected. The type of leadership that I make reference to here should be one of wisdom and love, not hostility.

Please don't forget to be a virtuous woman, to maintain a high standard of holiness, and to be without blame. Note that a virtuous woman is one who is trustworthy, reliable, and very supportive of her husband and family. Also, she is one who enables her husband to feel secure due to the virtue she possesses. She is wise, hardworking, and committed. In addition, she prepares food to feed her family, is quite thrifty, and gives to the poor. She is one who fears the Lord greatly.

Wives, remember that your external beauty is very important, and you should carry yourself modestly. However, your internal beauty is more important. Internal beauty is characterized by humility and a gentle spirit. I encourage you to be a carrier of these qualities. In the Garden of Eden, Eve was brought to Adam as a helpmate. Therefore, it is one of your duties as a wife to be instrumental in helping your husband to fulfill his purpose in God. This type of submission only comes with sacrificial love, and should not be done under duress. You should be willing to work cohesively with your spouse to fulfill purpose and destiny.

Being a wife, you must remain faithful to your husband, especially sexually. You have a duty to take care of his sexual needs and sexual gratification. This should help to deter him from seeking sexual gratification elsewhere. Although, let me pause to say, despite the fact that some husbands' sexual needs are being catered to by their wives, they still become weak and are led away by harlots. This is adultery that desecrates the sanctity of marriage. Your efforts to satisfy your husband are parallel to the Church and Christ. The onus is on both of you to keep this union clean. You made this covenant to each other at the altar, so if there is another in your marriage, it should be the Son of God. Marriage is not triangular in nature; rather, it is monogamous.

In addition, be wise and alert. Don't become a replica of Bathsheba, Delilah, or Jezebel. All these died a long time ago, but their spirits are still rampant in the lives of some females. This is unhealthy; don't let it be named among you. As a wife, you are responsible for dressing modestly. You should not allow yourself to be provocatively dressed nor to be seductive in public. If you do, then you are tempting other men to lust over you. A wife is expected to be of godly character, one who lives an exemplary life that portrays Christ. You should not be a brawler. You should be one whose children can call her blessed. The life of a godly wife is comparable to the life of the Church in relation to her groom, Jesus Christ.

Endeavour to work with your spouse collaboratively. Communicate respectfully with him. You are meant to be his closest companion, except for his relationship with God. As such, take the time to listen to him and try to understand him. Don't denigrate or belittle his manhood. You should be an emblem of purity, sanctification, and faithfulness to your groom. Women, you are also expected to put on the full armour of God and wear it with pride. Give no space to the devil to intercept your marriage. You also have the responsibility to guard it with prayer and fasting.

CHAPTER 10

ABUSE IN MARRIAGE

Marriage is plagued by different types of abuse, including physical, sexual, verbal, emotional, psychological, and financial abuse, to name a few. Many spouses are being abused due to drugs and alcohol use. Abuse in marriage is not only done to the spouse, but also extends to the children. Abuse can be defined as any uninvited behaviour that is controlling, with the intent to manipulate, exercise power over another, induce fear, or inflict pain or injury on its victim. It is also used to gain and sustain control over the victim's actions, belief system, and thoughts. Abuse is normally done by someone who is very close to the victim. For example, someone's current or ex-spouse, parents, or other relation.

Abuse is normally cyclical in nature. Its frequency and severity increase as it escalates. The tactics used are both systematic and intentional. Abuse should not have any place in your marriage with your spouse. If it is, then it is demonic and you should desist from doing it. God is not pleased with this type of behaviour. You have become one flesh, so when you abuse your spouse you are, in fact, abusing yourself.

Emotional and psychological abuse takes place when systematic behaviour or schemes are used to instill fear into someone and reduce or diminish their self-worth. It is also meant to humiliate, control, and intimidate a person. This is quite rampant in some marriages. Here, the abuser tends to put down the other spouse by derogatory name-calling or with the use of negative adjectives. Verbally, the abuser is normally aggressive, and there is an all-out assassination of the other person's self-esteem. The abused is sometimes denied easy access to personal affection or not permitted to practice proper personal care or hygiene.

There are cases where the abused spouse is not even allowed to be close to friends and family, or is given threats of publicizing false, derogatory information about themselves to friends, relatives, and the general public. The intention here is to isolate the abused person from vital social networks of friends and family that can offer moral support. At times, the victim is even limited in terms of whom he or she can talk to, or the duration of a phone call. This also includes forcible confinement.

Emotional and psychological abuse also occurs when great control is exercised over the other spouse's mode of dressing, hairstyle, haircut, among other things. There is also the issuance of threats of different types, including the threat of committing suicide, of harming the children, of involving Child Protective Services, or stalking and harassing the victim. Screaming and yelling at your spouse or even silently evading or isolating oneself is another form of emotional and psychological abuse, and should be stopped.

Spiritual Abuse occurs when a religious belief system is employed with the objective to denigrate or control another person. This also takes place in marriages, where one spouse uses certain religious beliefs to gain control over the other. It is sometimes used to inflict punishment on the victim. This type of abuse involves coercing the abused spouse to involuntarily be a part of a different religious group or cult. At times, the victim's religious beliefs are attacked, and they are not allowed to practice a different religious belief. They may also be hindered from attending certain places of worship; for example, a synagogue or church.

Sexual abuse is sexual activities that are not consented to, including unwanted sexual touching that are forced. The objective here is to carry out sexual acts that are painful, degrading, or humiliating. Surprisingly, this also takes place in marriages, because many spouses are forcefully engaging each other in sexually immoral activities, without consent. Many people are engaging in acts that are degrading, humiliating, and that cause much pain to their victim. For example, forcing one's spouse to be involved in group sex, spousal swap, rape, to terminate a pregnancy, or forcing the abused to watch or be actively engaged in pornography. Also, the denial of sex from the victim is abuse, and could include false accusation of infidelity.

Financial abuse is any act committed with the intention of maintaining excessive control over one's spouse. This type of abuse is very prevalent in marriages, yet it goes undetected or unnoticed. In some cases, ignorance is the reason but cannot be considered bliss. There are cases in which a spouse is denied access to valuable training or educational opportunities that could make them more marketable in the job market. These opportunities could possibly result in an increase in their earning potential and better employment. They are denied access to this type of education or training because the other spouse feels threatened that their spouse might become more financially independent. This denial of finances is done in order to make him or her less financially independent. Sometimes a man may feel inferior to his wife if she is more educationally qualified and is in a higher income bracket. Sometimes a spouse is even prevented from having a job, although it is necessary.

There are also cases of financial abuse where one spouse destroys the other's credit rating by racking up huge unpaid debts. At times, this is done without the knowledge of the other person or the owner of the credit cards. The family's disposable income or savings are at times misappropriated by one person, leading to severe poverty in some marriages. There are also times when spouses are spending the financial resources of the marriage in other areas that are not a part of the marriage, such as on people or things they should not be spending their money on. In addition, there are scenarios where excessive control is exercised over how and where the other spouse can spend money. At times, only one spouse is allowed to spend the disposable income of the family.

If you are withholding financial support and vital financial information in your marriage, this is financial abuse. This also comes in the form of a spouse not contributing financially to the union as they ought to, not because they are not able to do so, but for malicious reasons. Sometimes, it is so severe to the point where it affects the acquisition of life's most basic necessities, such as to purchase food, clothing, medication, or for emergency purposes.

To the man, let me remind you that from a biblical perspective, if you are not providing for your household, then you are "worse than one who is an infidel" (1 Timothy 5:8). Lastly, if you are overindulging in activities that assassinate and deplete the financial resources of your marriage, then this is financial abuse. Issuance of threats to cut off financial support or contribution in your marriage also signifies financial abuse.

Physical Abuse can be defined as the inflicting of pain and injury upon another, intentionally. This type of abuse is very common in lots of marriages and, sadly, is also seen by some as normal so many spouses remain quiet about it. Physical abuse is characterized by unwelcome, deliberate physical contact that is done with the intention to cause bodily harm or injury. This sometimes comes in the form of slapping, punching, kicking and, in extreme cases, stabbing or shooting. Many spouses have become casualties as a result of this devious type of behaviour from their partner.

In addition, there are cases where one spouse is ill and has to be cared for by the other spouse, but the care given is done in a negative way. Sometimes, the ill spouse is given too much or too little medication in contrast to the amount prescribed by a doctor. This has resulted in the sick spouse becoming over-medicated or under-medicated. This is wrong and ungodly, and must be strongly denounced. If you are guilty of this, God is not pleased with that type of behaviour. Very often, these abuses are induced by alcohol and drug use.

Verbal Abuse involves the use of words designed to denigrate someone and damage his or her self-esteem. It tends to belittle an individual, causing that person to see him or herself of lesser value. This can be a very subtle and controlling tool.

It is necessary that you learn how to communicate with your spouse. Disagreements will come, but you must learn how to disagree with each other respectfully, without any form of aggression. Be sure to take the time out to learn and master the art of conflict resolution.

Are You in an Abusive Relationship?

Abuse affects the dignity and self-worth, and dehumanizes and demoralizes the victim, causing them to feel worthless and deserving of this malicious and dirty act. Victims are caught in an emotional prison, practically being issued a life sentence, and held in a position where they cannot arise easily to explore and maximize their true potential. Therefore, it robs its victims of their potential.

Some souls are mangled for a lifetime and attract predators for life. The effects of abuse are deeply rooted, and cripple the victim. It retards or disables the developmental process of a child and permanently inflicts internal scars. These scars manifest themselves externally in many ways. Victims often go in pursuit of partners with characteristics of their abusers, causing a recurring cycle.

TO THE ABUSED

If you are being abused, I implore you to seek help on the initial onset of the abuse, be it verbal, physical, emotional, or financial. This should not be allowed to go untreated. If this is not rooted out from the seed, it will germinate and blossom into a tree. Remember, the tree cannot be bent when it is old; it has already grown.

If you are a wife who is being battered, you are only commissioned by God to submit to your husband in terms of honouring and obeying him; not to be walked on by him. He has no moral, spiritual, or legal right to be abusive. The Bible declares that the husband should be seen as the head of the wife. However, this doesn't mean that he should serve from the position of a bully. In fact, he should serve from a position of headship, taking care of his household. Also, he should be the head in the sense that he should be the vehicle through which wisdom, knowledge, and sound reasoning operate within the marriage. This does not mean he should be domineering and abusive. If dominance defines you, you need to change your thinking and adjust your attitude. In Ephesians 5:21, we are told that both wives and husbands should be submitting themselves to each other.

On the other hand, if you are a husband who is being abused, then God is not in agreement with this either. Both of you need to submit yourselves to each other. Men, you are commissioned to love your wives in like manner as Christ loves His Church. However, you are not supposed to be abused by your wife. You are supposed to be reverenced and cared for by her, not domineered and controlled.

TO THE ABUSER

Abuse in marriage transcends all geographical boundaries, races, ages, religions, cultures, and socio-economic groups. Whenever the covenant of marriage takes place, the two have been joined into one flesh. The question is, how can you delight in hurting your own flesh? This is ungodly and should not be practiced. Love thinks no evil. Instead, you should delight in nourishing and cherishing your "one flesh." If your spouse is hurting, you should also be hurting.

One of the most basic rights of a person is to live free from abuse. Each person in a marriage is entitled to be shown dignity and respect as a human being, and to enjoy the right to be safe, have proper emotional health, and have their most basic physiological needs met. In addition, they have a right to personal or professional development, and the necessary resources to facilitate these developments.

If you are an abuser, it is obvious that you need both spiritual help and professional counselling. Abuse is normally a long-standing problem that could have started way back into someone's childhood that wasn't dealt with properly. This exposure to abuse could either be as a victim or as an observer. Therefore, it could be deeply entrenched into one's behaviour. As a result, I implore you to get the necessary help to rid yourself of such evil. If you are the male abusing spouse, remember that one of your ribs was taken out from your side to form your wife. How then can you continue to hurt her? Aren't you supposed to be one flesh? Lack of love for your wife is a form of abuse from your position of headship.

However, if you are the female abusing spouse, you have no moral or legal grounds on which to stand regarding hurting your husband. Instead, you are commissioned in God's Word to submit yourself to your own husband.

CHAPTER 11

THE SANCTITY OF MARRIAGE

The word "sanctity" means to be godly and of a holy character. It also refers to being sacred, holy, and free from profanity. Therefore, the sanctity of marriage refers to marriage in accordance to God's divine will and order; a union that is holy, sacred, and does not violate God's divine purpose for it. In other words, a marriage that is in accordance with God's mandate. Marriage is holy and sanctified by God Himself. Hebrews 13:4 says, "Let marriage be held in honour among all, and let the marriage bed be undefiled, for God will judge the sexually immoral and adulterous." Sexual sin and impurities defile and defy the laws of God. In the Old Testament, it is evident that sexual purity in marriage is highly esteemed. It is serious to the extent that on the night of the marriage, if the bride was proven to be unfaithful, she would be returned to her parents and stoned to death. Whenever the sanctity of marriage was desecrated, it brought forth death, either spiritually or physically; for example, David and Bathsheba.

The sanctity of marriage is also desecrated whenever cohabitation takes place outside of marriage. God honours sexual purity. This helps to restore the sanctity of marriage and show one's appreciation for it.
Pay keen attention to the following:

➢ Matthew 5:31-32 says, "It has been said, 'Anyone who divorces his wife must give her a certificate of divorce. But I tell you that anyone who divorces his wife, except for sexual immorality, causes her to become an adulteress, and anyone who marries the divorced woman commits adultery."

➢ Adultery desecrates and defiles marriage. Therefore, it violates God's law and must not be taken for granted. In the case of Potiphar's wife, who tried to seduce Joseph into lying with her, Joseph refused to lie with her, not because he was a coward, but because he respected the sanctity of marriage. Joseph knew that adultery was wrong, and he didn't want to be a part of this evil, so he stood his ground.

➢ Not only do these types of impurities defile the persons involved, but also the land in which they live. The Canaanites in the Book of Leviticus were chased out of the land after their defilement.

➢ Abstain from sexual impurity and embrace sanctification in your marriage. That is what God requires. The apostle Paul adjured us to keep our vessels sanctified. This is indicative of sexual purity.

➢ The desecration of the sanctity of marriage has a deep spiritual truth, much to the contrary of the beliefs of many. Firstly, the Bible states that if you lie with a harlot, you have become one flesh with the harlot. Secondly, the marriage relationship draws great parallel to that relationship that exists between Christ and His Church. He is the Bridegroom and the Church is His Bride. Now, whenever the Church sins again God and goes after other gods, the Church is considered to be unfaithful, and God is not pleased with that. Throughout the Scriptures, the Church is warned not to go whoring with other gods.

Therefore, if you fail to embrace the sanctity of marriage, you are negatively affecting this covenant relationship from a spiritual, as well as a physical, standpoint. In Proverbs 5:15, you are instructed to "drink water from your own cistern." Men, you should be content with your own wife and you ought not to envy your neighbour's wife. Don't yield to the temptation of seeking sexual gratification outside of your marriage. Your spring should not be dispersed in the street or outside of your house.

Sexual impurity carries a chain reaction, and I will name a few below:
➢ Allows one to become immune to the things of God
➢ Severs your relationship with God and your spouse
➢ Destroys the very fabric of the family unit
➢ Causes a spiritual, and sometimes physical, death and leaves one susceptible to God's judgement
➢ Results in the defilement of oneself
➢ Causes one to sin against God.

There are many ways in which one can embrace the sanctity of marriage, such as:
➢ Abstaining from sexual sin and letting it not be named among you
➢ Letting every man have his own wife and deal with her accordingly
➢ Showing the high honour and respect that is due to marriage
➢ Viewing marriage in the way God sees it
➢ Becoming one flesh with your spouse
➢ Embracing sexual intimacy, which has a deep spiritual enshrinement
➢ Valuing your spouse as your helpmate and one whom God has given you for companionship
➢ Embracing procreation. This is one of the major reasons why God brought a man and woman into the covenant relationship of marriage.

The attacks on the sanctity of marriage are designed to destroy the *"seed."* If a farmer destroys or allows his seed to be destroyed, then he cannot experience a harvest. This principle also applies to marriage.

CONCLUSION

In conclusion, marriage is a covenant that is meant to be for life, except on the grounds of adultery or sexual immorality. It is for better, worse, sickness, and health. It is the only institution on Earth where a man and a woman can truly express their deepest longing for companionship, intimacy, and spirituality into oneness through the same medium. This is a very special type of relationship.

God designed marriage for the purposes of procreation, companionship, helping each other, relationship building, and joy. Therefore, enjoy each other's presence as you live as one. Stand firm in your marriage. Fight as a good soldier to protect it from thieves and murderers. Guard its gates with fasting and prayer. Don't lose sight of the fact that foreign bodies are only there to steal, kill, and destroy your marriage.

In this covenant, you both have a duty to God and to each other to guard the gates of your marriage and your family. Ensure that you don't leave this gate open, or else your marriage will be ravished and plundered by murderers and thieves. Hijackers are on a demonic assignment, orchestrated by Satan himself, to destroy this covenant relationship. They appear nicely packaged, yet their contents are highly lethal. They are like the forbidden fruit that was placed in the Garden of Eden. In case you don't know the full details of this story, let me take the time to relay it to you because of its level of importance. God placed a tree in the garden with forbidden fruit. However, He specifically instructed Adam and Eve not to eat any of the fruit, or else they would die. They became disobedient and ate the fruit. This was not God's will for them. Due to this disobedience, they severed their relationship with God, and mankind plunged into darkness. Not only did this affect both of them, but humanity was also negatively affected. The forbidden fruit of adultery has broken, and continues to break, this sacred, honourable, and covenant relationship. You will harvest more than what you sow, so be careful what you sow.

Finally, stand on guard as a good soldier for your marriage. Be vigilant, because Satan and his cohorts are fighting for your marriage to become another statistic of the divorce rate. Keep sending out missiles against the enemies of your marriage. You should not only be defensive, but also offensive. You must fight to win. To be indecisive and not fight, suggests that you have already surrendered, that you have already decided not to win.

I appreciate your time and willingness to embark on such an incredible journey through the pages of this book. My objectives are for you to find strength, encouragement, support, knowledge, and insight through the pages of this book. I admit that some of its contents could be considered explosive, but in a positive way. Don't forget that you are in a fight where missiles are being launched daily. Therefore, our weaponry must be explosive in combat. This is for our good and meant to help us not to "forget the ancient landmark" (Amos 7:7-9), for marriage was established from the foundations of the world by God Himself. Remember, He does not change. At the end of all of this, we should become better spouses.

AUTHOR BIOGRAPHY

While growing up, I gave my heart to the Lord and was saved at the tender age of nine years old. I was very much involved in the work of my local church. At the age of fourteen, I felt the call of God on my life and started ministering in the pulpit of my local church and its associate churches, especially on youth Sundays. I taught Sunday school, and sang both in the choir and as a soloist. During this time, I successfully represented my church in debates and competitions, annually. I dedicated my life to seek the lost at any cost.

Upon my arrival in Canada, God led me to a body of believers who were being led by a dedicated servant of God. During this time, God gave me two beautiful daughters. I worshipped at the Driftwood Church of God, now known as Covenant of Promise, in Toronto for ten years. I continued to be quite active in the work of God. My involvements at church included singing in the choir, and I served as the Assistant Youth Director for a period of time.

God then led me to my current place of worship. This congregation is being led by Bishop L. Walker, a visionary and dedicated servant of God. His unwavering faith and tenacity to live out God's purpose has helped to motivate me to stand firm on God's promises, even in the face of adversity. At my current place of worship, I continue to serve God and fulfil His mandate upon my life. Here, I once served as a member of the outreach team and presently as a member of the sanctuary choir.

In the last few years, I have encountered many storms in my life, but I stood on the promises of God, knowing that I could not and cannot be defeated. God's words take pre-eminence in my life, and I am a winner. Despite the many pains and hardships I have experienced, I have not become bitter. Instead, everything that was meant to destroy me has become a catalyst for my success in God and for the fulfilment of my destiny. I continue to strive for greatness in the kingdom of God daily, leaving the negatives behind me.

I now hold a B.A. in Psychology and am currently enrolled in a combined Master's and PhD program at a Theological Seminary in Florida, where I am doing a clinical study in Christian Marriage and Family Counselling. I currently work as a Civil Servant with a major municipality. My desire is to serve God and to walk daily according to His precepts and council. In fulfilling my true destiny and purpose for being on Earth, I will leave an indelible mark on society at the end of my journey. That is the true duty of mankind.